4.99

Negotiating with the Dead
A Writer on Writing

What is the role of the writer? Prophe... Jester? Or witness to the real world? ...hood and the development of her wr... examines the metaphors which writers of fiction and p... to explain – or excuse! – their activities, looking at what costumes they have seen fit to assume, what roles they have chosen to play. In her final chapter she takes up the challenge of the book's title: if a writer is to be seen as 'gifted,' who is doing the giving and what are the terms of the gift?

Margaret Atwood's wide and eclectic reference to other writers, living and dead, is balanced by anecdotes from her own experiences as a writer, both in Canada and on the international scene. The lightness of her touch is underlined by a seriousness about the purpose and the pleasures of writing, and by a deep familiarity with the myths and traditions of Western literature.

Margaret Atwood was born in 1939 in Ottawa and grew up in northern Quebec, Ontario, and Toronto. She received her undergraduate degree from Victoria College at the University of Toronto and her master's degree from Radcliffe College.

Throughout her thirty years of writing, Margaret Atwood has received numerous awards and honorary degrees. She is the author of more than twenty-five volumes of poetry, fiction, and non-fiction and is perhaps best known for her novels, which include *The Edible Woman* (1969), *Surfacing* (1972), *The Handmaid's Tale* (1985), *Cat's Eye* (1988), *The Robber Bride* (1993), and *Alias Grace* (1996). Her newest novel, *The Blind Assassin*, won the 2000 Booker Prize for Fiction.

Margaret Atwood has been acclaimed for her talent for portraying both personal lives and problems of universal concern. Her work has been published in more than thirty-five languages, including Japanese, Turkish, Finnish, Korean, Icelandic and Estonian.

Negotiating with the Dead

A Writer on Writing

MARGARET ATWOOD

Virago

A *Virago* Book

Published by Virago Press 2003

First published by Cambridge University Press 2002
This paperback edition is published with the permission
of the Syndicate of the Press of the University of Cambridge,
Cambridge, England

A CIP catalogue record for this book is available from the British Library

ISBN 1 84408 027 7

Typeset in Adobe Garamond by M Rules
Printed and bound in Great Britain by
Clays Ltd, St Ives plc.

Virago Press
An imprint of
Time Warner Books UK
Brettenham House
Lancaster Place
London WC2E 7EN

www.virago.co.uk

The Empson Lectures

The Empson Lectures, named after the great scholar and literary critic Sir William Empson (1906–84), have been established by the University of Cambridge as a series designed to address topics of broad literary and cultural interest. Sponsored jointly by the Faculty of English and Cambridge University Press, the series provides a unique forum for distinguished writers and scholars of international reputation to explore wide-ranging literary–cultural themes in an accessible manner.

As they were all sitting at table, one guest suggested that each of them should relate a tale. Then the bridegroom said to the bride: 'Come, my dear, do you know nothing? Relate something to us, like the others.' She said: 'Then I will relate a dream.'

> 'The Robber Bridegroom,' collected by the
> Brothers Grimm[1]

. . . I moot reherce
Hir tales alle, be they bettre or werse,
Or elles falsen som of my mateere.
And therefore, whoso list it nat yheere,
Turne over the leef and chese another tale . . .

> Geoffrey Chaucer, *The Canterbury Tales*[2]

And now in imagination he has climbed
another planet, the better to look
with single camera view upon this earth –
its total scope, and each afflated tick,
its talk, its trick, its tracklessness – and this,
this he would like to write down in a book!

> A. M. Klein, 'Portrait of the Poet as Landscape'[3]

For the others

Contents

Introduction: **Into the labyrinth**

The act of naming is the great and solemn consolation of mankind.

Elias Canetti, *The Agony of Flies* [1]

I still do not know what impels anyone sound of mind to leave dry land and spend a lifetime describing people who do not exist. If it is child's play, an extension of make believe – something one is frequently assured by people who write about writing – how to account for the overriding wish to do that, just that, only that, and consider it as rational an occupation as riding a bicycle over the Alps?

Mavis Gallant, Preface, *Selected Stories* [2]

Finding yourself in a hole, at the bottom of a hole, in almost total solitude, and discovering that only writing can save you. To be without the slightest subject for a book, the slightest idea for a book, is to find yourself, once again, before a book. A vast emptiness. A possible book. Before nothing. Before something like living, naked writing, like something terrible, terrible to overcome.

Marguerite Duras, *Writing* [3]

When I was a student of English literature, in the early 1960s, we all had to read an important critical text called *Seven Types of Ambiguity* (1930). This erudite book, it is astonishing to note, was written by William Empson when he was only twenty-three. It is also astonishing to note that when he was in the full throes of composition he was expelled from the University of Cambridge for being found with contraceptives in his room.

This is a fitting commentary on how we are all stuck in time, less like flies in amber – nothing so hard and clear – but like mice in molasses; because surely nowadays he would be expelled for being found *without* contraceptives in his room. The twenty-three-year-old William Empson sounds like a wise and considerate youth as well as an energetic one, and one who did not give up in the face of discouragement, and so when I was requested to give the Empson Lectures at the University of Cambridge for the year 2000 – a series of six, to be delivered to an audience composed not only of scholars and students, but also of the general public – I was more than delighted.

Or rather, I was more than delighted when first asked – such undertakings always seem so easy and pleasant two years ahead – but as the time for actually giving the lectures approached, I became less delighted by the day.

The broad subject proposed was, more or less, Writing, or Being a Writer, and since I've done that and been one, you'd think I'd have something to say. I thought so too; what I had in mind was a grand scheme in which I would examine the various self-images – the job descriptions, if you like – that writers have constructed for themselves over the years. I would do this in a way that was not too technical, and would contain no more obscure references than I felt were really necessary; and I would throw in some of my own invaluable experiences and insights along the way, thereby not only striking a 'personal note,' as fraudulent journalists in Henry James stories used to say, but also illuminating the entire field in a striking and original way.

However, as time passed, my initial grandiose but cloudy visions dispersed, leaving a kind of daunted blankness. It was like finding yourself in a great library as a young writer, and gazing around at the thousands of books in it, and wondering if you really have anything of value to add.

The more I thought about this the worse it became. Writing itself is always bad enough, but writing about writing is surely worse, in the futility department. You don't even have the usual excuse of fiction – namely, that you are just making things up and therefore can't be held to any hard-and-fast standards of verisimilitude. Perhaps the auditors, and then the readers – you arrogantly assume there will be some – will want literary theories, or abstract plans, or declarations, or manifestos, and then you open the theory-and-manifesto drawer and find it empty. Or at least I did. And then what?

I will pass over the frenzied scribblings that followed, adding only that I found myself as usual behind deadline, and – an even greater obstacle – in Madrid, where some of the books I had confidently expected to find in the English sections of bookstores were not there (including – somewhat witheringly – my own).

Despite these obstacles, the lectures were stapled together somehow, and delivered. The parts where profound thought and the
results of decades of painstaking scholarship were replaced by
sticky tape and string are not supposed to be noticeable.

This book grew out of those lectures. It is about writing, although
it isn't about how to write; nor is it about my own writing; nor is
it about the writing of any person or age or country in particular.
How to describe it? Let's say it's about the position the writer
finds himself in; or herself, which is always a little different. It's the
sort of book a person who's been laboring in the wordmines for,
say, forty years – by coincidence, roughly the time I myself have
been doing this – the book such a person might think of beginning, the day after he or she wakes up in the middle of the night
and wonders what she's been up to all this time.

What has she been up to, and why, and for whom? And what
is this *writing*, anyway, as a human activity or as a vocation, or as
a profession, or as a hack job, or perhaps even as an art, and why
do so many people feel compelled to do it? In what way is it different from – for instance – painting or composing or singing or
dancing or acting? And how have other people who have done
this thing viewed their own activity, and themselves in relation to
it? And are their views of any comfort? And has the concept of
the writer *qua* writer, as expounded by (of course) writers,
changed at all over the years? And what exactly do we mean
when we say *a writer*? What sort of creature do we have in mind?
Is the writer the unacknowledged legislator of the world,[4] as
Shelley so grandiosely proclaimed, or is he one of Carlyle's blimp-
like Great Men, or is he the snivelling neurotic wreck and
ineffectual weenie so beloved of his contemporary biographers?

Or perhaps I intended a warning for the unsuspecting young.
Perhaps I have written about the subjects in this book not only

because they were things about which I was anxious at the outset of my own writing life, but because many people – judging from the questions they ask – continue to be anxious about them today. Perhaps I have reached the age at which those who have been through the wash-and-spin cycle a few times become seized by the notion that their own experience in the suds may be relevant to others. Perhaps I wish to say: *Look behind you. You are not alone. Don't permit yourself to be ambushed. Watch out for the snakes. Watch out for the* Zeitgeist – *it is not always your friend. Keats was not killed by a bad review. Get back on the horse that threw you.* Advice for the innocent pilgrim, worthy enough, no doubt, but no doubt useless: dangers multiply by the hour, you never step into the same river twice, the vast empty spaces of the blank page appall, and everyone walks into the maze blindfolded.

I'll begin with the standard disclaimer. I am a writer and a reader, and that's about it. I'm not a scholar or a literary theoretician, and any such notions that have wandered into this book have got there by the usual writerly methods, which resemble the ways of the jackdaw: we steal the shiny bits, and build them into the structures of our own disorderly nests.

In an early short story by poet James Reaney, the narrator watches his sister feeding the hens by spelling out words with the hen-feed, letter by letter. He says, 'I often wondered to whom she was writing, up there in the sky.'[5] The primate narrator of Ian McEwan's short story, 'Reflections of a Kept Ape,' is also watching a writer writing. He ponders, not the potential reader, but the potential motive, though he comes to no very cheering conclusion. 'Was art then nothing more than a wish to appear busy?' he muses. 'Was it nothing more than a fear of silence, of boredom, which the merely reiterative rattle of the typewriter's keys was enough to allay?'[6]

'I wonder where it all comes from?' asked Reena, a thirty-four-year-old woman who has been writing since the age of six and throwing it all into the waste basket, but who thinks she may now be almost ready to begin.[7]

These are the three questions most often posed to writers, both by readers and by themselves: *Who are you writing for? Why do you do it? Where does it come from?*

While I was writing these pages, I began compiling a list of answers to one of these questions – the question about motive. Some of these answers may appear to you to be more serious than others, but they are all real, and there is nothing to prevent a writer from being propelled by several of them at once, or indeed by all. They are taken from the words of writers themselves – retrieved from such dubious sources as newspaper interviews and autobiographies, but also recorded live from conversations in the backs of bookstores before the dreaded group signing, or between bites in cut-rate hamburger joints and tapas bars and other such writerly haunts, or in the obscure corners of receptions given to honor other, more prominent writers; but also from the words of fictional writers – all written of course by writers – though these are sometimes disguised in works of fiction as painters or composers or other artistic folk. Here then is the list:

To record the world as it is. To set down the past before it is all forgotten. To excavate the past *because* it has been forgotten. To satisfy my desire for revenge. Because I knew I had to keep writing or else I would die. Because to write is to take risks, and it is only by taking risks that we know we are alive. To produce order out of chaos. To delight and instruct (not often found after the early twentieth century, or not in that form). To please myself. To express myself. To express myself beautifully. To create a perfect work of art. To reward the virtuous and punish the guilty; or – the Marquis de Sade defense, used by ironists – vice versa. To hold a mirror up to Nature. To hold a mirror up to the reader. To paint a portrait of society and its ills. To express the unexpressed life of the masses. To name the hitherto unnamed. To defend the human spirit, and human integrity and honor. To thumb my nose at Death. To make money so my children could have shoes. To make money so I could sneer at those who formerly sneered at me. To show the bastards. Because to create is human. Because to create is Godlike. Because I hated the idea of having a job. To say a new word. To make a new thing. To create a national consciousness, or a national conscience. To justify my failures in school. To justify my own view of myself and my life, because I couldn't be 'a writer' unless I actually did some writing. To make myself appear more interesting than I actually was. To attract the love of a beautiful woman. To attract the love of any woman at all. To attract the love of a beautiful man. To rectify the imperfections of my miserable childhood. To thwart my parents. To spin a fascinating tale. To amuse and please the reader. To amuse and please myself. To pass the time, even though it would have passed anyway. Graphomania. Compulsive logorrhea. Because I was driven to it by some force outside my control. Because I was possessed. Because an angel dictated to me. Because I fell into the embrace of the Muse. Because I got pregnant by the Muse and needed to give birth to a book (an interesting piece of cross-dressing, indulged in by male writers of the seventeenth century). Because I had books instead of children (several twentieth-century women). To serve Art. To serve the Collective Unconscious. To serve History. To justify the ways of God toward man. To act out antisocial behavior for which I would have been punished in real life. To master a craft so I could generate texts (a recent entry). To subvert the Establishment. To demonstrate that whatever is, is right. To experiment with new forms of perception. To create a recreational boudoir so the reader could go into it and have fun (translated from a Czech newspaper).

Because the story took hold of me and wouldn't let me go (the Ancient Mariner defense). To search for understanding of the reader and myself. To cope with my depression. For my children. To make a name that would survive death. To defend a minority group or oppressed class. To speak for those who cannot speak for themselves. To expose appalling wrongs or atrocities. To record the times through which I have lived. To bear witness to horrifying events that I have survived. To speak for the dead. To celebrate life in all its complexity. To praise the universe. To allow for the possibility of hope and redemption. To give back something of what has been given to me.

Evidently, any search for a clutch of common motives would prove fruitless: the *sine qua non*, the essential nugget without which writing would not be itself, was not to be found there. Mavis Gallant begins the Preface to her *Selected Stories* with a shorter and more sophisticated list of writers' motives, beginning with Samuel Beckett, who said writing was all he was good for, and ending with the Polish poet Aleksander Wat, who told her that it was like the story of the camel and the Bedouin: in the end, the camel takes over. 'So that was the writing life:' she comments, 'an insistent camel.'[8]

Having failed on the subject of motives, I took a different approach: instead of asking other writers why they did it, I asked them what it felt like. Specifically, I asked novelists, and I asked them what it felt like when they went into a novel.

None of them wanted to know what I meant by *into*. One said it was like walking into a labyrinth, without knowing what monster might be inside; another said it was like groping through a tunnel; another said it was like being in a cave – she could see daylight through the opening, but she herself was in darkness.

Another said it was like being under water, in a lake or ocean. Another said it was like being in a completely dark room, feeling her way: she had to rearrange the furniture in the dark, and then when it was all arranged the light would come on. Another said it was like wading through a deep river, at dawn or twilight; another said it was like being in an empty room which was nevertheless filled with unspoken words, with a sort of whispering; another said it was like grappling with an unseen being or entity; another said it was like sitting in an empty theatre before any play or film had started, waiting for the characters to appear.

Dante begins the *Divine Comedy* – which is both a poem and a record of the composition of that poem – with an account of finding himself in a dark, tangled wood, at night, having lost his way, after which the sun begins to rise. Virginia Woolf said that writing a novel is like walking through a dark room, holding a lantern which lights up what is already in the room anyway. Margaret Laurence and others have said that it is like Jacob wrestling with his angel in the night – an act in which wounding, naming, and blessing all take place at once.

Obstruction, obscurity, emptiness, disorientation, twilight, blackout, often combined with a struggle or path or journey – an inability to see one's way forward, but a feeling that there was a way forward, and that the act of going forward would eventually bring about the conditions for vision – these were the common elements in many descriptions of the process of writing. I was reminded of something a medical student said to me about the interior of the human body, forty years ago: 'It's dark in there.'

Possibly, then, writing has to do with darkness, and a desire or perhaps a compulsion to enter it, and, with luck, to illuminate it, and to bring something back out to the light. This book is about that kind of darkness, and that kind of desire.

Prologue

This book began life as a series of six lectures, intended for a mixed audience: young and not so young, men and women, specialists in literature and students, general readers, and – especially – writers at an earlier stage or dewier age than my own. In converting these pieces from the spoken to the written word I have attempted to retain the colloquial tone, although I admit to having removed some of the cornier jokes. Those who were present will realize that some material has migrated from here to there, and that several passages have been expanded and – I hope – clarified. The grab-bag nature of the citations is, however, a feature of the inside of my head, and despite all efforts to make this locale tidier, nothing much could be done about it. The eccentricities of taste and judgment are my own.

The book has inherited its shape from its progenitors; thus the organization of chapters is not tightly sequential. One chapter does not lead by a direct pathway into the next, though all circle around a set of common themes having to do with the writer, her medium, and his art.

The first chapter is the most autobiographical, and also indicates the range of my references: these two things are connected, as writers tend to adopt their terms of discourse early in their reading and writing lives. The second chapter deals with the post-Romantic writer's double consciousness: I assume that we are still living in the shadow cast by the Romantic movement, or in the fragments of that shadow. The third chapter treats the conflict between the gods of art and those of commerce that every writer who considers himself an artist still feels; the fourth considers the writer as illusionist, artificer, and participant in social and political power. The fifth chapter probes that eternal triangle: writer, book, and reader. And the sixth and last is about the narrative journey and its dark and winding ways.

In short, this book struggles with a number of the conflicts that have occupied many writers, both those I have known on this plane of earthly being, as they say in California, and those I have known only through their work. Between a rock and a hard place is where much writing is carried on, and these are some of the rocks, and some of the hard places.

I would like to thank my kind and generous hosts at Clare Hall, Dame Gillian Beer and her husband, Dr. John Beer, who made my stay at Cambridge so pleasant; also Claire Daunton, who was in charge of organizing me there. Dr. Sally Bushell took care of my spatial orientation, and Professor Ian Donaldson of the English Department and his wife Grazia Gunn provided a warm and convivial evening. Dr. Germaine Greer must always be thanked on general principles, and for her courage and good humor; as must Xandra Bingley, ever true.

At Cambridge University Press, Sarah Stanton has been the long-suffering editor, with Margaret Berrill acting as copy-editor and Valerie Elliston as indexer. Andrew Brown is the Press Academic Director.

Many thanks as well to Vivienne Schuster, my agent at Curtis Brown in London, and to Euan Thorneycroft, her dauntless backup; and to my other agents, Phoebe Larmore and Diana

MacKay, who, though not directly involved in this book, have kept a watchful eye on me lest I run out to play in the traffic. On the Toronto end, thanks to the intrepid Sarah Cooper and to Jennifer Osti, my once and future assistants, and to Sarah Webster, who so assiduously helped with the research and footnotes. Edna Slater called my attention to the 1948 article by Earle Birney cited in chapter 1; and Martha Butterfield must also be thanked, for reasons having to do with the Brown Owl you will encounter in chapter 5.

Finally, thank you to my family – to my sons Matt and Grae, who have dealt with their wicked stepmother over the years with grace and skill; to my daughter Jess Gibson, avid reader, always ready to plunge fearlessly into a new and perilous text; and to Graeme Gibson, whose love, support, and companionship over the years have sustained me in my precarious and somewhat tatty Palace of Art.

And to my teachers, including the inadvertent ones, as always.

1

Orientation:
Who do you think you are?
What is 'a writer,' and how did I become one?

. . . a colony lacks the spiritual energy to rise above routine, and . . . it lacks this energy because it does not adequately believe in itself . . . It sets the great good place not in its present, nor in its past nor in its future, but somewhere outside its own borders, somewhere beyond its own possibilities . . . A great art is fostered by artists and audience possessing in common a passionate and peculiar interest in the kind of life that exists in the country where they live.

    E. K. Brown, 'The Problem of a Canadian Literature' (1943)[1]

. . . if you should throw a poetry contest with a prize big enough to attract five hundred poets . . . you might feel that putting them all together you'd arrive at the typical Canadian maker. When you have finished reading the five hundred poems what you find is that about three people have come close to getting the thing, I mean they know how to write poetry professionally . . . After these three you get about two hundred metrical smoothies without a metaphor in their bones and then three hundred metrical hobblers . . . Flying in and out of this mass are three or four poems brilliant and eerie and spine-chilling because these are the poems of mad people . . . This analysis of the five hundred Canadian poets fills me with gloom because it represents the grass roots poet, poetry reader, and average sensitive citizen in this country and he is just not very literary at all.

> James Reaney, 'The Canadian Poet's Predicament' (1957)[2]

The Canadian poet has all the models in the language (not to mention other languages) at his disposal, but lacks the deadening awareness that he is competing with them.

> Milton Wilson, 'Other Canadians and After' (1958)[3]

– it seemed that I had to be a writer as well as a reader. I bought a school notebook and tried to write – did write, pages that started off authoritatively and then went dry, so that I had to tear them out and twist them up in hard punishment and put them in the garbage can. I did this over and over again until I had only the notebook cover left. Then I bought another notebook and started the whole process once more. The same cycle – excitement and despair, excitement and despair.

> Alice Munro, 'Cortes Island' (1999)[4]

Writing, Writers, The Writing Life – if this last is not an oxymoron. Is this subject like the many-headed Hydra, which grows two other subtexts as soon as you demolish one? Or is it more like Jacob's nameless angel, with whom you must wrestle until he blesses you? Or is it like Proteus, who must be firmly grasped through all his changes? Hard to get hold of, certainly. Where to start? At the end called Writing, or the end called The Writer? With the gerund or the noun, the activity or the one performing it? And where exactly does one stop and the other begin?

In the novel *The Woman in the Dunes*,[5] by the Japanese writer Kobo Abé, a man called Nikki finds himself trapped against his will at the bottom of a huge sandpit, along with a solitary woman, where he is forced to shovel away the sand that keeps sifting down on them. To comfort himself in his hopeless predicament, he considers writing about his ordeal. 'Why couldn't he observe things in a more self-possessed way? If and when he got back safely it would certainly be well worthwhile setting down this experience.'

Then a second voice enters his head, and he begins a dialogue with it.

"'– Well, Nikki . . .'" it says. "'At last you have decided to write something. It really was the experience that made you . . .'"

"'– Thanks. Actually I've got to think up some kind of title.'"

You see, Nikki has already slipped into the role of writer – he recognizes the importance of *the title*. A few steps more and he'd be pondering the cover design. But he soon loses confidence, and declares that no matter how he tries, he's not fit to be a writer. The second voice then reassures him: "'There's no need for you to think of writers as something special. If you write, you're a writer, aren't you?'"

Apparently not, says Nikki. "'Saying you want to become a writer is no more than egotism; you want to distinguish between yourself and the puppets by making yourself a puppeteer.'"

The voice says this is too severe. "'. . . certainly you should be able to distinguish . . . between being a writer and writing.'"

"'– Ah. You see!'" says Nikki. "'That's the very reason I wanted to become a writer. If I couldn't be a writer there would be no particular need to write!'"

Writing – the setting down of words – is an ordinary enough activity, and according to Nikki's second voice there's nothing very mysterious about it. Anyone literate can take an implement in hand and make marks on a flat surface. *Being a writer*, however, seems to be a socially acknowledged role, and one that carries some sort of weight or impressive significance – we hear a capital W on *Writer*. Nikki's reason for wanting to write is that he wants the status – he wants to cut a figure in society. But happy the writer who begins simply with the activity itself – the defacement of blank pieces of paper – without having first encountered the socially acknowledged role. It is not always a particularly blissful or fortunate role to find yourself saddled with, and it comes with a price; though, like many roles, it can lend a certain kind of power to those who assume the costume.

But the costume varies. Every child is born, not only to specific parents, within a specific language and climate and political situation, but also into a pre-existing matrix of opinions about children – whether they should be seen and not heard, whether sparing the rod spoils them, whether they should be praised every day so they won't develop negative self-esteem, and so forth. So also it is with writers. No writer emerges from childhood into a pristine environment, free from other people's biases about writers. All of us bump up against a number of preconceptions about what we are or ought to be like, what constitutes good writing, and what social functions writing fulfills, or ought to fulfill. All of us develop our own ideas about what we are writing in relation to these preconceptions. Whether we attempt to live up to them, rebel against them, or find others using them to judge us, they affect our lives as writers.

I myself grew up in a society that, at first glance, might have seemed to lack any such preconceptions. Certainly writing and art were not the foremost topics of daily conversation in Canada when I was born – in 1939, two and a half months after the outbreak of World War II. People had other things on their minds, and even if they hadn't, they wouldn't have been thinking about writers. In a magazine article published nine years later entitled 'Canadians Can Read, But Do They?' the poet Earle Birney claimed that most Canadians had only three hardcover books in the house: the Bible, the works of Shakespeare, and Fitzgerald's *The Rubáiyát of Omar Khayyám*.

My parents were both from Nova Scotia, a province from which they felt themselves in exile all their lives. My father was born in 1906, and was the son of a backwoods farmer. His mother had been a schoolteacher, and it was she who encouraged my father to educate himself – through correspondence courses, there being no high school within reach. He then went to

Normal School, taught primary school, saved the money from that, got a scholarship, worked in lumber camps, lived in tents during the summers, cooked his own food, cleaned out rabbit hutches at a low wage, managed at the same time to send enough money 'home' to put his three sisters through high school, and ended up with a doctorate in Forest Entomology. As you might deduce, he believed in self-sufficiency, and Henry David Thoreau was one of the writers he admired.

My mother's father was a country doctor of the kind that drove a sleigh and team through blizzards to deliver babies on kitchen tables. She herself was a tomboy who loved riding horses and ice-skating, had scant use for housework, walked barn ridge-poles, and practiced her piano pieces – since various efforts were made to turn her into a lady – with a novel open on her knees. My father saw her sliding down a banister at Normal School and decided then and there that she was the girl he would marry.

By the time I was born, my father was running a tiny forest-insect research station in northern Québec. Every spring my parents would take off for the North; every autumn, when the snow set in, they would return to a city – usually to a different apartment each time. At the age of six months, I was carried into the woods in a packsack, and this landscape became my hometown.

The childhoods of writers are thought to have something to do with their vocation, but when you look at these childhoods they are in fact very different. What they often contain, however, are books and solitude, and my own childhood was right on track. There were no films or theatres in the North, and the radio didn't work very well. But there were always books. I learned to read early, was an avid reader and read everything I could get my hands on – no one ever told me I couldn't read a book. My mother liked quietness in children, and a child who is reading is very quiet.

Because none of my relatives were people I could actually see, my own grandmothers were no more and no less mythological than Little Red Riding Hood's grandmother, and perhaps this had something to do with my eventual writing life – the inability to distinguish between the real and the imagined, or rather the attitude that what we consider real is also imagined: every life lived is also an inner life, a life created.

A good many writers have had isolated childhoods; a good many have also had storytellers in their lives. My primal storyteller was my brother; at first I featured only as audience, but soon was allowed to join in. The rule was that you kept going until you ran out of ideas or just wanted a turn at being the listener. Our main saga involved a race of supernatural animals that lived on a distant planet. An ignorant person might have mistaken these for rabbits, but they were ruthless carnivores and could fly through the air. These stories were adventures: war, weapons, enemies and allies, hidden treasure, and daring escapes were the main features.

Stories were for twilight, and when it was raining; the rest of the time, life was brisk and practical. There was very little said about moral and social misdemeanors – we didn't have much opportunity for them. We did get instructions about avoiding lethal stupidity – don't set forest fires, don't fall out of boats, don't go swimming in thunderstorms – that sort of thing. Because my father built everything – the cabins we lived in, our furniture, boat docks, and so forth – we had free access to hammers, saws, rasps, drills, brace-and-bits, and dangerous edged tools of every kind, and we played with them a lot. Eventually we were taught the sensible way to clean a gun (take the bullets out first, don't look down the barrel from the front end) and how to kill a fish quickly (knife blade between the eyes). Squeamishness and whining were not encouraged; girls were not expected to do more of it than boys; crying was not viewed with indulgence. Rational debate was smiled upon, as was curiosity about almost everything.

But deep down I was not a rationalist. I was the youngest and weepiest of the family, frequently sent for naps due to fatigue, and thought to be sensitive and even a bit sickly; perhaps this was because I showed an undue interest in sissy stuff like knitting and dresses and stuffed bunnies. My own view of myself was that I was small and innocuous, a marshmallow compared to the others. I was a poor shot with a 22, for instance, and not very good with an ax. It took me a long time to figure out that the youngest in a family of dragons is still a dragon from the point of view of those who find dragons alarming.

I was five in 1945, when the War ended and balloons and colored comics returned. This was a time when I began to have more to do with cities, and with other people. The postwar housing boom was underway, and the house we now lived in was one of the new split-level boxes. My bedroom was painted a soft peach, which was a first – no other bedroom I'd ever slept in had had paint on the walls. I also went to school for the first time, during the winter months. Having to sit at a desk all day made me tired, and I was sent for more naps than ever.

Around the age of seven I wrote a play. The protagonist was a giant; the theme was crime and punishment; the crime was lying, as befits a future novelist; the punishment was being squashed to death by the moon. But who was to perform this masterpiece? I couldn't be all the characters at once. My solution was puppets. I made the characters out of paper, and a stage from a cardboard box.

This play was not a raging success. As I recall, my brother and his pals came in and laughed at it, thus giving me an early experience of literary criticism. I stopped writing plays, and began a novel; but I never got past the opening scene, in which the main character – an ant – was being swept downriver on a raft. Perhaps the demands of a longer form were too much for me. In any case I stopped writing then, and forgot all about it. I took to painting instead, and drawing pictures of fashionable ladies, smoking cigarettes in holders and wearing fancy gowns and very high heels.

When I was eight we moved again, to another postwar bungalow, this time nearer the center of Toronto, at that time a stodgy provincial city of seven hundred thousand. I was now faced with real life, in the form of other little girls – their prudery and snobbery, their Byzantine social life based on whispering and vicious gossip, and an inability to pick up earthworms without wriggling all over and making mewing noises like a kitten. I was more familiar with the forthright mindset of boys: the rope burn on the wrist and the dead-finger trick were familiar to me – but little girls were almost an alien species. I was very curious about them, and remain so.

By now it was the late 1940s. Women, no longer required for wartime production, had been herded back into the home, and the Baby Boom was on: marriage and four kids were the ideal, and remained so for the next fifteen years. Canada was such a cultural backwater that we didn't get the full force of this ideology – there were still some adventurous Amelia Earhart types left over, still some bluestockings, still some independent and even radical women who'd come through the thirties and forties and had always supported themselves; but smoothly run domesticity was the approved trend.

Underneath all this was a sublayer of fear: the atomic bomb had exploded, the Cold War was on, Joe McCarthy had begun his Red-bashing; it was important to look as normal, as ordinary, as non-Communist as possible. It occurred to me that my parents, once the measure of sanity and reasonableness, might be viewed by others as eccentric; perhaps no worse than harmless loonies, but possibly atheists, or unsound in some other way. I did try to be like everyone else, though I didn't have much idea what 'everyone else' was supposed to be like.

I turned ten in 1949, the age of Patti Page, the Singing Rage, who harmonized with herself on the first double-track recording I ever heard: I was becoming corrupted by popular culture, much to my parents' dismay. This was the age of sniffling radio soap-operas, of night-time serials such as *The Green Hornet* and *Inner Sanctum*, and of magazine advertisements that played up the germ scare and urged homemakers to go to war on dirt. Pimples, bad breath, dandruff, and body odor were other ills that plagued the population, and I was fascinated by the ads on the backs of comics – tales of social failure redeemed by a tube of toothpaste, or fables about Charles Atlas, whose body-building exercises would keep bullies from kicking sand in your face at the beach.

I read the complete works of Edgar Allan Poe at this time: Poe was in the school library, as he did not deal with sex and was therefore considered suitable for children. I was addicted to the works of E. Nesbit, and I read all the Andrew Lang folk-tale collections I could find. I had no use for Nancy Drew, the girl detective – she was too wholesome for me – but I fell in love with Sherlock Holmes at the age of twelve, a hopeless but safe passion.

By this time I was in high school, at far too young an age. Children could skip grades then, but could not leave school until the age of sixteen, so I found myself in a class full of large people who shaved. I responded by developing anemia and an odd noise in my heart, and by going to sleep a lot. But then the next year I grew somewhat, and all those with leather jackets, motorcycles, and bicycle chains concealed under their socks had left, and I had been given fried liver and iron pills to pep me up, so you might say things had improved somewhat.

I was fifteen when Elvis Presley made his début: thus I could both waltz and rock-and-roll, but missed the tango, which was not then fashionable. This was the era of sock hops, of going steady, of drive-in movies, of well-meant articles by grownups about the dangers of necking and petting. There was no sex education at our school – the gym teacher even spelled the word *blood* instead of pronouncing it outright, lest girls faint at the sound of it. The Pill was far in the future. Girls who got pregnant disappeared from sight. Either they'd undergone abortions which had killed or mangled them, or they'd had shotgun weddings and were washing diapers, or else they were hidden away in Homes for Unwed Mothers, where they were put to work scrubbing floors. This was a fate that needed at all costs to be avoided, and rubber panti-girdles were right on hand to help you avoid it. The entire culture seemed geared – as many have been before it – to ceaseless titillation coupled with a high brick wall.

However, I learned many things about the seedier side of life via the printed page. My reading up until the age of sixteen was wide but indiscriminate – everything from Jane Austen to True Romance magazines to pulp science fiction to *Moby Dick* – but it divided generally into three kinds of books: books read in school as part of the course, acceptable books read openly outside of school – found lying around the house or got from the library – and books suspected of being taboo, peeked at while baby-sitting for careless neighbors – which is how I got my hands on *Forever Amber* and *The Blackboard Jungle*, this last a hymn to the hazards of transparent nylon blouses.

The most horrifying of these books was *Peyton Place* bought furtively at the corner store and read on top of the garage roof, which could be reached by a ladder and was conveniently flat. The heroine of this book wanted to be a writer, but what she had to go through to become one was nauseating in the extreme.

Never mind – she certainly had lots of material to write about. Incest, venereal disease, rape, varicose veins – it was all in there.

In school, by contrast, the curriculum was determinedly British, and just as determinedly pre-modern. I assume this was to avoid any onstage sex, though there was lots of it offstage, both as act and as possibility, and usually ending in disaster – *Romeo and Juliet*, *The Mill on the Floss*, *Tess of the d'Urbervilles*, *The Mayor of Casterbridge*. There was plenty of poetry. Teaching focused on the texts, and on the texts alone. We learned to memorize these texts, analyze their structure and style, and make précis of them, but none of them were placed in a historical or biographical context. I suppose this was the spillover from the New Criticism, though nobody mentioned that term; and nobody talked about writing as a process or a profession – as something real people actually did.

Given such conditions, how is it that I became a writer? It wasn't a likely thing for me to have done, nor was it something I chose, as you might choose to be a lawyer or a dentist. It simply happened, suddenly, in 1956, while I was crossing the football field on the way home from school. I wrote a poem in my head and then I wrote it down, and after that writing was the only thing I wanted to do. I didn't know that this poem of mine wasn't at all good, and if I had known, I probably wouldn't have cared. It wasn't the result but the experience that had hooked me: it was the electricity. My transition from not being a writer to being one was instantaneous, like the change from docile bank clerk to fanged monster in 'B' movies. Anyone looking might have thought I'd been exposed to some chemical or cosmic ray of the kind that causes rats to become gigantic or men to become invisible.

I wasn't old enough to be at all self-conscious about what had just happened to me. If I'd read more about writers' lives, or indeed anything at all about them, I would have concealed the shameful transformation that had just taken place in me. Instead I announced it, much to the shock of the group of girls with whom I ate my paper-bag lunches in the high-school cafeteria. One of them has since told me that she thought I was very brave to just *come out* with something like that; she thought I had a lot of nerve. In truth I was simply ignorant.

There was also, as it turned out, the dismay of my parents to be reckoned with: their tolerance about caterpillars and beetles and other non-human life forms did not quite extend to artists. As was their habit, they bit their tongues and decided to wait out what they hoped would be a phase, and made oblique suggestions about the necessity of having a paying job. One of my mother's friends was more cheerful. 'That's nice, dear,' she said, 'because at least you'll be able to do it at home.' (She assumed that, like all right-thinking girls, I would eventually have a home. She wasn't up on the current dirt about female writers, and did not know that these stern and dedicated creatures were supposed to forgo all of that, in favor of warped virginity or seedy loose living, or suicide – suffering of one kind or another.)

If I had suspected anything about the role I would be expected to fulfill, not just as a writer, but as a *female* writer – how irrevocably doomed! – I would have flung my leaky blue blob-making ballpoint pen across the room, or plastered myself over with an impenetrable *nom de plume*, like B. Traven, author of *The Treasure of the Sierra Madre*, whose true identity has never been discovered. Or, like Thomas Pynchon, I would never have done any interviews, nor allowed my photo to appear on book jackets; but I was too young then to know about such ruses, and by now it is far too late.

In biographies there is usually some determining moment in early life that predicts the course of the future artist or scientist or politician. The child must be father to the man, and if he isn't,

the biographer will do some cut-and-paste and stick on a different head, to make it all come out right. We do so wish to believe
in a logical universe. But when I look back over the life I led until
I began writing, I can find nothing in it that would account for
the bizarre direction I took; or nothing that couldn't be found in
the lives of many people who did not become writers.

When I published my first real collection of poetry at the age
of twenty-six – 'real' as opposed to the small pamphlet I myself
had printed up on a flat-bed press in a friend's cellar, as was the
fashion among poets in those days – my brother wrote to me,
'Congratulations on publishing your first book of poetry. I used
to do that kind of thing myself when I was younger.' And perhaps that is the clue. We shared many of the same childhood
pursuits, but he gave them up and turned to other forms of
amusement, and I did not.

There I was, then, in 1956, still at high school, without a soul in
sight who shared my view of what I should, could, and ought to
be doing. I did not know anyone who was a writer, except my
aunt, who wrote children's stories for Sunday-school magazines,
which to my snobbish young mind did not count. None of the
novelists whose books I had read – none that wrote for adults,
that is, whether trashy books or literary ones – were alive and
living in Canada. I had not yet seriously begun to search for
others of my kind, to ferret them out of their damp caves and
secret groves, so my view at the age of sixteen was that of the general citizen: I could see only what was made clearly visible to me.
It was as if the public role of the writer – a role taken for granted,
it seemed, in other countries and at other times, had either never
become established in Canada, or had existed once but had
become extinct. To quote A. M. Klein's 'Portrait of the Poet as
Landscape' – a poem I had not yet read, but was to stumble

upon shortly and to imprint on, much as a newly hatched duck
may imprint on a kangaroo –

> It is possible that he is dead, and not discovered.
> It is possible that he can be found some place
> In a narrow closet, like a corpse in a detective story,
> Standing, his eyes staring, and ready to fall on his face . . .
>
> We are sure only that from our real society
> He has disappeared; he simply does not count . . .
>
> . . . is, if he is at all, a number, an x,
> a Mr. Smith in a hotel register, –
> incognito, lost, lacunal.[6]

My first idea about writing was that I would write gushy romantic stories for pulp magazines – these paid good money, so *Writers'
Markets* informed me – and live off the avails while writing serious
literature; but a couple of tries at it convinced me that I lacked the
vocabulary. My next idea was that I should go to journalism school
and then work for a newspaper; I thought one kind of writing
might lead to another – the kind I wanted to do, which by now
had become a blend of Katherine Mansfield and Ernest
Hemingway. But after I had talked to a real journalist – a second
cousin my parents dredged up to discourage me – I changed my
mind, because he told me that as a girl I would be put to work
writing the obituaries and the ladies' pages, and nothing else. So,
having passed the examinations that were the gateway to university,
and about which I still have nightmares, off I went. Once I had
graduated I could teach something or other, I supposed. That
wouldn't be too bad because there would be a long summer vacation, during which I could compose my masterpieces.

I was seventeen; the year was 1957. Our professors let it be

known that we were a dull lot, not nearly as exciting as the war
vets who'd come back a decade earlier, filled with hard experience
and lusting for knowledge, and not as exciting either as the left-
ies who'd caused so much ferment in the thirties, when they
themselves had been at university. They were right: by and large,
we were a dull lot. The boys were headed for the professions, the
girls for futures as their wives. The first wore grey flannels and
blazers and ties, the second camel-hair coats, cashmere twin-sets,
and pearl button earrings.

But there were also the others. The others wore black turtle-
necks and – if girls – black ballerina leotards under their skirts,
panti-hose not having been invented yet and skirts being manda-
tory. These others were few in number, often brilliant, considered
pretentious, and referred to as 'artsy-fartsies.' At first they terrified
me, and then, a couple of years later, I in turn terrified others.
You didn't have to do anything in particular to inspire this terror:
you just had to understand a certain range of likes and dislikes,
and to look a certain way – less manicured, paler in the face,
gaunter, and of course more somber in your clothing, like
Hamlet – all of which implied you could think thoughts too eso-
teric for ordinary people to understand. Normal youths sneered
at the artsies, at least at the male ones, and sometimes threw
them into snow banks. Girls of an artistic bent were assumed to
be more sexually available than the cashmere twin-set ones, but
also mouthier, crazier, meaner, and subject to tantrums: getting
involved with one was therefore more trouble than the sex might
be worth.

What the artsy-fartsies were interested in was not Canadian
literature, or not at first; like everyone else, they barely knew it
existed. Jack Kerouac and the Beat Generation had hit the scene
in the late 1950s and were well known through the pages of *Life*
magazine, but they hadn't made as much of a dint in the artsies

as you might suppose: our interests were more European. You were supposed to be familiar with Faulkner and Scott Fitzgerald and Hemingway, and Tennessee Williams and Eugene O'Neill for the dramatically inclined, and the Steinbeck of *Grapes of Wrath*, and Whitman and Dickinson to a certain extent, and Henry Miller for those who could get hold of a smuggled copy – his works were banned – and James Baldwin for the civil rights crowd, and Eliot and Pound and Joyce and Woolf and Yeats and so forth as a matter of course, but Kierkegaard, *Steppenwolf*, Samuel Beckett, Albert Camus, Jean-Paul Sartre, Franz Kafka, Ionesco, Brecht, Heinrich Böll, and Pirandello were the magic names. Flaubert, Proust, Baudelaire, Gide, Zola, and the great Russians – Tolstoy, Dostoevsky – were read by some. Occasionally, to shock, someone would claim to like Ayn Rand: it was thought to be daring that the hero rapes the heroine and the heroine enjoys it, though that was in fact the subtext of a good many Hollywood movies featuring spats, slaps in the face, slammed doors, and clinches at the end.

For a country that was supposed to be such a colony, so firmly – still – in the cultural grip of the crumbling British Empire, contemporary British writers had a fairly small toehold. George Orwell was dead, but read; so was Dylan Thomas. Doris Lessing's *Golden Notebook* was admitted to by a few very formidable women, and read in secret by a lot more. Iris Murdoch was just starting out, and was considered weird enough to be of interest; Graham Greene was still alive, and was respected, though not as much as he was later to become. Christopher Isherwood had a certain cachet because he had been in Germany when the Nazis were on the rise. The Irish writer Flann O'Brien had a small but devoted following, as did Connolly's *The Unquiet Grave*. The real British impact was being felt through a subversive radio program called *The Goon Show*, which had Peter Sellers in it, and another Monty Python precursor called *Beyond the Fringe*, known through – as I recall – a recording of it.

The first artistic group I got involved with was the theatre folk. I didn't want to be an actress, but I knew how to paint sets, and could be dragged in to act, in minor parts, in a pinch. For a while I designed and printed theatre posters as an alternative to working in a drugstore; I wasn't really very good at it, but then, there wasn't much competition. The artsy group was small, like the artsy group in Canada itself, and everyone connected with it usually fiddled around in more than one field of activity. I was also pals with the folk-singers – collecting authentic ballads and playing such instruments as the autoharp were in style – and through them I absorbed a surprisingly large repertoire of plangent lovers' laments and murderous gore-filled plots, and truly filthy ditties.

All of this time I had been writing, compulsively, badly, hopefully. I wrote in almost every form I have since written – poems, fiction, non-fiction prose – and then I laboriously typed these pieces out, using all four of the fingers I have continued to employ until this day. In the college reading room I was able to obsess over the few thin literary magazines – I think there were five – then published in the country in English, and wonder why the poems in them might be judged by some white-bearded, Godlike editor to be better than mine.

After a while I began publishing in the campus literary magazines, and then – via a self-addressed, stamped envelope, the secret of which I had learned from *Writers' Markets* – in one of the thin, desirable five. (I used my initials instead of a first name – I didn't want anyone important to know I was a girl. Anyway, in high school we'd studied an essay by Sir Arthur Quiller-Couch which said that the 'masculine' style was bold, strong, vivid, and so forth, and the 'feminine' one was pastel, vapid, and simpy. Writers are fond of saying that writers are androgynous as to their capabilities, and that is no doubt true, though it is telling that most of those who make this claim are women. But they are not gender-neutral in their interests. Most importantly, they are treated differently, especially by reviewers, however that difference in treatment may manifest itself; and sooner or later that will affect them.)

When I received my first literary-magazine acceptance letter, I walked around in a daze for a week. It was a shock, really. All that effort directed toward what even I had, in my heart of hearts, considered to be an unreal goal, and now it was not unreal after all. Everything was about to come true, as in some vaguely threat-ening dream or wish-granting fairy-tale. I'd read too much folklore – gold that turned to coal in the morning, beauty that caused your hands to be cut off – not to know that there would now be trickery and hazards, and some hidden, potentially lethal price to be paid.

Through the literary magazines, and also through some of my professors, who wrote for them, I discovered a concealed door. It was like a door in a bare hill – a tumulus in winter, or an anthill. Outside, to the uninformed observer, there was no life to be seen; but if you'd found the door and managed to make your way inside, all was furious motion. There was a whole microcosm of literary activity going on, as it were, right under my nose.

It seems that poets did exist, in Canada; they existed in small clumps, and even in schools – the 'cosmopolitan,' the 'native.' They denied they belonged to these schools, and then attacked other poets for being in them; also they attacked the critics, most of whom were their fellow poets. They called one another scato-logical names; they wrote blurbs and reviewed one another's books, stroking their friends and knackering their enemies, just

as in literary histories about the eighteenth century; they pontif-
icated and uttered manifestos; they fell upon the thorns of life;
they bled.

There were several factors that added to the ferment at that
time. Northrop Frye, a professor at the very college in which I
was enrolled, had just published *The Anatomy of Criticism*
(1957), which had caused quite a stir not only at home but
abroad, and had set off a spate of roaring among the poets, who
quickly divided themselves into pro-myth and anti-myth fac-
tions. It was Frye who made a revolutionary statement –
revolutionary not just for Canada but for any society, especially
any colonial society: '. . . the center of reality is wherever one
happens to be, and its circumference is whatever one's imagination can make sense of.'[7] (So you didn't have to be from London
or Paris or New York after all!) Just down the road at an adjacent
college was Marshall McLuhan; he published *The Gutenberg
Galaxy* in 1960, causing another stir, this time about the media
and their effects on perception, and the possible obsolescence of
the written word. (So writers in London and Paris and New York
were in just as much trouble as us provincials!)

The yelling over myth and media and literature in general
was mostly done by poets. Novelists and short-story writers,
unlike the poets, had not yet grouped themselves into clumps
and palships. There were very few published Canadian novelists,
few knew one another, and of these many were living in other
countries, having gone there because they did not think they
could function as artists in Canada. A lot of the names that
would become familiar in the later sixties and the seventies –
Margaret Laurence, Mordecai Richler, Alice Munro, Marian
Engel, Graeme Gibson, Michael Ondaatje, Timothy Findley,
Rudy Wiebe – had yet to put in a definitive appearance.

I found that it was quite a lot easier than I'd thought to get into the magic anthill – the place where people other than your-self might think you were a writer, and might also accept this as a desirable thing to be. There was at that time a real bohemia – a layer of society apart from, and very different from, the rest of it – and once you were in it, you were in.

There was, for instance, a coffee-house called The Bohemian Embassy, situated in a falling-apart factory building, where poets congregated once a week to read their poems out loud. Once I had 'published,' I too was asked to do this. It was, I found, quite different from acting. Other people's words were a screen, a dis-guise, but to get up and read my own words – such an exposed position, such possibilities for making an idiot of yourself – this made me sick. (The 'poetry reading' was rapidly becoming an accepted thing to do, and would shortly be an expected one. Little did I know I had ten years of behind-the-scenes throwing-up to look forward to.)

These coffee-house gatherings were remarkable in many ways. One thing about them was their promiscuity, by which I mean the extreme kinds of mixture that took place there. Younger and older, male and female, published and not yet, established and neophyte, raving socialist and tense formalist, all mingled together at the tables with checked tablecloths and the manda-tory Chianti-bottle candle-holders.

Another thing was – how can I put this? It was borne in on me that some of these people – even the published ones, even the respected ones – weren't very good. Some were wonderful at times, but uneven; others read the same poems at every event; others were insufferably mannerist; others were clearly there mostly to pick up women, or men. Could it be that getting through the door into the swarming poetic anthill wasn't neces-sarily a guarantee of anything? What then was the true Certificate of Approval? How would you ever know whether you'd made the grade or not, and what was the grade, anyway? If some of these people were deluded about their talents – and it was clear they were – was it possible that I might be, as well? And come to think of it, what was 'good'? And who determined that, and what litmus paper did they use?

I'll leave myself there, back in 1961, twenty-one years old, biting my fingers and just beginning to realize what I'd got myself into, and return to writing as an art, and to the writer as the inheritor and bearer of a set of social assumptions about art in general, and about writing in particular.

There's one characteristic that sets writing apart from most of the other arts – its apparent democracy, by which I mean its availability to almost everyone as a medium of expression. As a recurring newspaper advertisement puts it, 'Why Not Be A Writer? . . . No previous experience or special education required.' Or as Elmore Leonard has one of his street crooks say,

> . . . You asking me . . . do I know how to write down
> words on a piece of paper? That's what you do, man, you
> put down one word after another as it comes in your
> head . . . You already learned in school how to write,
> didn't you? I *hope* so. You have the idea and you put
> down what you want to say. Then you get somebody to
> add in the commas and shit where they belong . . . There
> people do that for you.[8]

To be an opera singer you not only have to have a voice, you have to train for years; to be a composer you have to have an ear, to be a dancer you have to have a fit body, to act on the stage you have to be able to remember your lines, and so on. Being a visual artist now approaches writing, as regards its apparent easiness – when you hear remarks like 'My four-year-old could do better,' you know that envy and contempt are setting in, of the kind that stem from the belief that the artist in question is not really talented, only lucky or a slick operator, and probably a fraud as well. This is likely to happen when people can no longer see what gift or unusual ability sets an artist apart.

As for writing, most people secretly believe they themselves have a book in them, which they would write if they could only find the time. And there's some truth to this notion. A lot of people do have a book in them – that is, they have had an experience that other people might want to read about. But this is not the same as 'being a writer.'

Or, to put it in a more sinister way: everyone can dig a hole in a cemetery, but not everyone is a grave-digger. The latter takes a good deal more stamina and persistence. It is also, because of the nature of the activity, a deeply symbolic role. As a grave-digger, you are not just a person who excavates. You carry upon your shoulders the weight of other people's projections, of their fears and fantasies and anxieties and superstitions. You represent mortality, whether you like it or not. And so it is with any public role, including that of the Writer, capital W; but also as with any public role, the significance of that role – its emotional and symbolic content – varies over time.

The title of this chapter was borrowed from a 1978 collection of short stories by Alice Munro. In Canada this book was called *Who Do You Think You Are?*[9] but the British publishers changed it to *Rose and Flo* and the American publishers to *The Beggar Maid*. Presumably these other publishers thought the original title was somewhat obscure for their respective audiences; but it was all too comprehensible to any Canadian reader of the time, especially any reader who had ever had artistic aspirations.

The book is a *Bildungsroman* – an account of the youth and education – of a girl called Rose, who grows up to be a minor actress. As a girl, she attends a rough small-town Canadian high school, and the English class is set the task of copying out and then memorizing a poem. Rose has a talent for this and is able to recite the poem immediately, without having first done the copying. 'What did [Rose] expect to follow?' asks Munro. 'Astonishment, and compliments, and unaccustomed respect?' Yes, but that isn't what she gets. The teacher concludes that Rose has been showing off, which is true enough. '"Well, you may know the poem,"' she says, '"but that is no excuse for not doing what you were told. Sit down and write it in your book. I want you to write every line three times. If you don't get finished you can stay after four."' Rose does have to stay after four, and when she hands in the copy the teacher says, '"You can't go thinking you are better than other people just because you can learn poems. Who do you think you are?"'[10] In other words, Rose is not to believe she can escape from the common herd just because she can do some tricky, inessential thing most people can't.

For *actress*, read *writer*; for memorizing a poem, read composing a story. The teacher's attitude is one that all artists in the Western society of the past two hundred years, but especially those in smaller and more provincial places, have found themselves up against. Indeed, they have repeatedly formulated a series of questions about this very issue, along the lines of the dialogue I began with – the one between Nikki and his inner voice in *The Woman in the Dunes*. Is the writer – the writer who aspires to be not just a provider of newspaper copy or an adept at formula fiction, but an artist – is such a person special, and if so, how?

2

Duplicity:
The jekyll hand, the hyde hand, and the slippery double
Why there are always two

But when thou doest alms, let not they left hand know
what thy right hand doeth;
   That thine alms may be in secret; and thy Father
which seeth in secret himself shall reward thee openly.
   Matthew 6: 3–4

Bards of passion and of mirth,
Ye have left your souls on earth!
Have ye souls in heaven too,
Double-lived in regions new?
   John Keats, 'Bards of Passion and of Mirth'

. . . you have the jekyll hand, you have the hyde hand . . .
   Gwendolyn MacEwen, 'The Left Hand and
   Hiroshima'[1]

Powers of observation heightened beyond the normal
imply extraordinary disinvolvement: or rather the double
process, excessive preoccupation and identification with
the lives of others, and at the same time a monstrous
detachment . . . The tension between standing apart and
being fully involved: that is what makes a writer.
   Nadine Gordimer, Introduction, *Selected Stories*[2]

I grew up in a world of doubles. My generation of children had no television – ours was the age of comic books – and in these, a superhero was nobody unless he had an alter ego who really *was* nobody. Superman was really the bespectacled Clark Kent, Captain Marvel was really the crippled newsboy Billy Batson, Batman was really a Scarlet Pimpernel sort of fellow who acted a playboy twit in 'real life' – or was it the other way around? I understood these people at the emotional level – every child did. The superhero, large and powerful and good, was what we wished to be; the 'real' alias, the one who lived *dans le vrai* and was small and weak and fallible and at the mercy of beings more powerful than us, was what we actually were. Yeats and his theory of personae had nothing on us.

Little did we know that our superheroes were – among other things – projections cast by the setting sun of the Romantic movement. Yes, there were earlier examples of disguises and doubles. Yes, Odysseus disguised himself to re-enter his halls in Ithaca; yes, in the Christian religion God came to earth as Jesus of Nazareth, a poor carpenter. Yes, Odin and Zeus and St. Peter wander the world as beggars in legend and fairy-tale, rewarding those who treat them well, settling the hash of those who don't. But it was the Romantics, *par excellence*, who fixed this doubleness in the popular consciousness as a thing to be expected, and expected above all of artists.

Isaiah Berlin, in *The Roots of Romanticism*,[3] has done a much better job than I ever could of spelling out the differences between the 'enlightenment' writer or artist in the eighteenth century – servant of universal ideas, upholder of the establishment, patronized by the powers that be – and the Romantic version, as popularized (among other places) in the Puccini opera *La Bohème* – rebellious, poor, not for hire. Them in their garrets, starving and creating works of genius; the rest of society stuffing itself at its materialistic dining table, burping and ignoring them. Yet it is the artists who possess the secret identities, the secret powers, and – if posterity goes their way – the last laugh. There is so much more to them than there seems!

As for the artists who are also writers, they are doubles twice times over, for the mere act of writing splits the self into two. In this chapter, it is therefore the doubleness of the writer *qua* writer I will discuss.

I've always been intrigued by Browning's nightmarish poem, 'Childe Roland to the Dark Tower Came.' The narrator is Childe Roland, who has undertaken a quest, the object of which is never specified, though we assume it's not the Holy Grail. Usually in a quest you have some worthy object in view – something to find, something to gain – and many difficulties to overcome along the way, and so it must be with Childe Roland. But his quest becomes more hopeless and squalid with every step he takes. An old man jeers at him – this is always a bad sign, in quests – and courage gives way to despair as the landscape he travels through becomes more and more blighted and swamp-like. Finally, when he's least expecting it, there is the Dark Tower itself, and he sees he's been caught in a trap: the landscape has closed in on him and there's no way out. Not only that, but all around him are the ghosts of those who have gone before him on the same quest, and have failed, and are now waiting for him to do the same, and he realizes his quest is doomed.

The Tower is a threatening structure, squat and impenetrable and unique in the world, we are told; and hanging on it is something called a slug-horn. This is a bothersome musical instrument; Browning probably got the word from Chatterton, who used it to mean 'trumpet,' and I expect Browning liked the suggestively disgusting sound of it because it fitted in with the rest of the scenery. Anyway, the slug-horn is what you must blow to challenge whoever or whatever lives in the Dark Tower: some kind of monster, we strongly suspect.

Childe Roland's Dark Tower is – I feel – like Winston Smith's Room 101 in George Orwell's novel *Nineteen Eighty-Four*: it holds for each individual what that person most fears. Let's take it as a working hypothesis that Childe Roland is a writer – that is, a stand-in for Robert Browning himself – and that the quest is a quest in search of the as yet unwritten poem called 'Childe Roland to the Dark Tower Came,' and that the monster inside the Dark Tower is Childe Roland himself, in his poem-writing aspect. Here is my evidence. First, Browning wrote the poem in one go. It wasn't a project, it was – if you like – an overwhelming impulse, and such impulses usually come from the deepest part of the writing self. Second, it was inspired by three lines of Shakespeare's, from the blasted heath or mad scene in *King Lear*:

> Childe Rowland to the Dark Tower came:
> His word was still – 'Fie, foh, and fum,
> I smell the blood of a British man.'[4]

As we remember from childhood, this is what the giant says in 'Jack the Giant-Killer' and similar stories. But in Shakespeare's

lines, it is Childe Roland himself who speaks them. Therefore –
for Browning when he was reading the lines, and then writing the
poem – Childe Roland is his own giant. But he is also his own
giant-killer. He is thus his own murderous double.

And so, when the fatal slug-horn is blown, the monster who is
also Childe Roland comes out of the Tower, and matter and anti-
matter merge, and the quest is accomplished, because the poem,
'Childe Roland to the Dark Tower Came,' is now finished. The
last lines of the poem are: 'Dauntless the slug-horn to my lips
I set / And blew. "Childe Roland to the Dark Tower Came."'5
The hero thus vanishes into the last line of the poem named after
him, which is the same as the title. Paradoxically, then, the fore-
doomed failed quest has not failed after all – since its goal was the
composition of the poem, and the poem has in fact been composed – and even though Childe Roland – both manifestations of
him – has been evaporated by its completion, he will continue to
exist inside the poem he himself has just written. If that makes
you dizzy, think of the second of the Alice books, *Through the
Looking Glass*, and Alice's question – *who dreamed it?*

What is the relationship between the two entities we lump under
one name, that of 'the writer'? The particular writer. By *two*, I
mean the person who exists when no writing is going forward –
the one who walks the dog, eats bran for regularity, takes the car
in to be washed, and so forth – and that other, more shadowy
and altogether more equivocal personage who shares the same
body, and who, when no one is looking, takes it over and uses it
to commit the actual writing.

There's an epigram tacked to my office bulletin board,
pinched from a magazine – 'Wanting to meet an author because
you like his work is like wanting to meet a duck because you like
pâté.' That's a light enough comment upon the disappointments

of encountering the famous, or even the moderately well-known – they are always shorter and older and more ordinary than you expected – but there's a more sinister way of looking at it as well. In order for the pâté to be made and then eaten, the duck must first be killed. And who is it that does the killing?

Now, what disembodied hand or invisible monster just wrote that cold-blooded comment? Surely it wasn't me; I am a nice, cosy sort of person, a bit absent-minded, a dab hand at cookies, beloved by domestic animals, and a knitter of sweaters with arms that are too long. Anyway, that cold-blooded comment was a couple of lines ago. That was then, this is now, you never step twice into the same paragraph, and when I typed out that sentence I wasn't myself.

Who was I then? My evil twin or slippery double, perhaps. I am after all a writer, so it would follow as the day the night that I must have a slippery double – or at best a mildly dysfunctional one – stashed away somewhere. I've read more than one review of books with our joint surname on them that would go far toward suggesting that this other person – the one credited with authorship – is certainly not me. She could never be imagined – for instance – turning out a nicely browned loaf of oatmeal-and-molasses bread, whereas I . . . but that's another story.

You might say I was fated to be a writer – either that, or a con-artist or a spy or some other kind of criminal – because I was endowed at birth with a double identity. Due to the romanticism of my father, I was named after my mother; but then there were two of us, so I had to be called something else. Thus I grew up with a nickname, which had no legal validity, while my real name – if it can be called that – sat on my birth certificate, unknown to me, ticking away like a time-bomb. What a revelation it was for me to discover that I was not who I was! And that

I had another identity lurking out of sight, like an empty suitcase stashed in a closet, waiting to be filled.

Waste not, want not – I was bound to do something with this extra name of mine, sooner or later. My earliest work was published in high-school magazines, under my nickname; then there was a transitional period, during which I resorted to initials. Then, finally – and after being told by someone older than me that no one would take me seriously as a writer if I stuck to my nickname, and that initials had been used up for ever by T. S. Eliot – I caved in to Fate, and embraced my doubleness. The author is the name on the books. I'm the other one.

All writers are double, for the simple reason that you can never actually meet the author of the book you have just read. Too much time has elapsed between composition and publication, and the person who wrote the book is now a different person. Or so goes the alibi. On the one hand, this is a convenient way for a writer to wriggle out of responsibility, and you should pay no attention to it. Yet on the other hand, it is quite true.

You see how quickly we have begun talking about hands – two of them. Dexter and sinister. There has been a widespread suspicion among writers – widespread over at least the past century and a half – that there are two of him sharing the same body, with a hard-to-predict and difficult-to-pinpoint moment during which the one turns into the other. When writers have spoken consciously of their own double natures, they're likely to say that one half does the living, the other half the writing, and – if of a melancholy turn of mind – that each is parasitic upon the other. Still, like Peter Schlemihl,[6] who sells his shadow to the Devil and then realizes that without it he no longer has a valid existence, the relationship is symbiotic as well. The double may be shadowy, but it is also indispensable.

I should interpose here that not all doubles are bad news. Some can be noble self-sacrificing substitutes, as in the Brothers Grimm's tale 'The Gold Children,' the Kurosawa film *The Shadow Warrior*, and the Rossellini film *Il Generale Della Rovere*, the sultan-and-beggar duo in Isak Dinesen's 'A Consolatory Tale,' and the two sisters in Christina Rossetti's poem 'Goblin Market.' In 'good double' stories, however, both 'halves' are as bound together as they are in 'bad double' stories: on the fate of one depends the fate of the other.

Here is Daryl Hine on the subject of doubleness, from his poem, 'The Doppelgänger':

> So split and halved and twain is every part,
> So like two persons severed by a glass
> Which darkens the discerning *whose is whose*
> And gives two arms for love and two for hate,
> That they cannot discover what they're at
> And sometimes think of killing and embrace . . .[7]

The speaker, or speakers – there are perhaps two – identifies himself as a poet. Or at least one half is a poet. But which, if either, is 'real'?

Where does it come from, this notion that the writing self – the self that comes to be thought of as 'the author' – is not the same as the one who does the living? Where do writers pick up the idea that they have an alien of some sort living in their brain? Surely it wasn't Charles Dickens the fun-loving paterfamilias, keen deviser of Christmas games for his kiddies, who caused poor Little Nell[8] to die an early death? He cried the whole time his pen-wielding hand was pitilessly doing her in. No, it was the necrophiliac he carried around inside himself, like a tapeworm made of ink.

As E. L. Doctorow says in his latest novel, *City of God*, 'Migod, there is no one more dangerous than the storyteller.'⁹ Here is the Danish writer Isak Dinesen, describing the transformation in an otherwise insignificant man as soon as he assumes the mantle of narration: '"Yes, I can tell you a story," he said. During this time, although he kept so quiet, he was changed; the prim bailiff faded away, and in his place sat a deep and dangerous little figure, consolidated, alert and ruthless – the story-teller of all the ages.'¹⁰ I would say Isak Dinesen had read her *Dr. Jekyll and Mr. Hyde*, except that she wouldn't have to have read it, since this kind of transmutation would have been one she was already familiar with from her own experience. As a person she was Karen Blixen; as a writer of fiction, she was Isak Dinesen. Like several other women writers, she went Dr. Jekyll one better and got a sex change into the bargain.

Dr. Jekyll and Mr. Hyde owes something to old werewolf stories – the ordinary man who is transformed into a fanged madcap, given the right conditions – but it also owes a great deal to old stories about the *Doppelgänger*. Robert Louis Stevenson was far from being the first to have taken an interest in this species of duplicity. Identical twins – not quite the same thing as doubles – have always attracted attention. In some African societies they were killed, to ward off bad luck, and we still find something uncanny about them: perhaps such exact replication suggests to us a denial of our own uniqueness.

I remember twins first catching my attention through an advertisement in a magazine, when I was twelve. This advertisement was for a home permanent known as a Toni, and it showed two identical girls, each with waved hair. The slogan was, 'Which Twin has the Toni?' – the idea being that one of them had a cheap home perm and the other one had an expensive salon job, and nobody could tell the difference. Why was it that I suspected fraud? Perhaps because of the suggestion that one twin was somehow the original – the authentic, the real thing – of which the other was merely a copy.

Twins and doubles are a very old motif in mythologies. Usually they are male – Jacob and Esau, Romulus and Remus, Cain and Abel, Osiris and Set – and often they struggle for dominance. They can be associated with the founding of a city or a people, though often one twin or double does not fare so well as the other. In his book on human sacrifice, *The Highest Altar*,[11] Patrick Tierney would have it that the successful twin represents the living society, and the unsuccessful one his dark alter ego – the one who was sacrificed and then buried under the cornerstone in order to deal with the Underworld, propitiate the gods, and protect the city.

Twins or twin-like siblings continued to exert a fascination into the age of 'literature' – Shakespeare's good Edgar and bad Edmund, in *King Lear*, or, for less drastic effect, the two sets of identical masters and servants in *The Comedy of Errors*. But the double is more than a twin or sibling. He or she is *you*, a you who shares your most essential features – your appearance, your voice, even your name – and, in traditional societies, such doubles were usually bad luck. According to Scottish folklore, to meet your own double was a sign of death: the double was a 'fetch,' come from the land of the dead to collect you.[12] The ancient Greek story of Narcissus may be connected with a similar superstition about seeing your double: what Narcissus sees is his own reflection – himself, but a self on the other side of the watery mirror – and it lures him to his death.

Those who have taken an interest in the Salem witch trials in seventeenth-century New England will be familiar with the concept of 'spectral evidence,' which was accorded the same legal status as more tangible exhibits, such as wax effigies stuck full of pins. Witches were supposed to have the ability to send out their 'specter,' or incorporeal likeness, to do their dirty work for them. Thus if someone saw you in the barnyard hexing the cows and you could demonstrate by witnesses that you were home in bed at the time, what was proven was not your innocence, but the fact that you had the ability to project your own double, and were therefore a witch. (It was not until spectral evidence was barred from the courts that the New England witchcraft trials finally ended.)

Among the things that fascinated the early Romantics were folk-stories and folklore, so it is perhaps through this door that so many doubles got into the literature of the Romantic and post-Romantic periods. The atmosphere of these 'double' stories and their many descendants is usually delirium and terror – as movie-goers will recognize if they've seen, for instance, such 'double' films as *The Stepford Wives*, *The Other*, or *Dead Ringers*. One of the earliest English-language literary 'double' stories of this type is James Hogg's *Confessions of a Justified Sinner* (1824), in which the protagonist – convinced he's predestined to salvation, and is therefore free to sin as he likes – wakes from what he thinks is a long sleep to find that a man who looks just like him has been doing nasty things, for which he himself will have to take the blame. Poe's story 'William Wilson' (1839) is similar: the pro-tagonist is haunted by a man with the same name who looks exactly like him, and who functions as an interfering conscience. Our hero ends by killing the other William Wilson, thereby killing himself: like Dr. Jekyll and Mr. Hyde, the two William Wilsons share their mortality, and one cannot exist without the other. Later in the nineteenth century, Henry James has a more psychological 'double' story: in 'The Jolly Corner' (1909) an American aesthete returns from Europe, and becomes convinced that his former house is inhabited, not by an exact replica of him-self, but by the ghost of what he would have been if he'd stayed in America and become a rich tycoon. He stalks this shadow, finally confronts it, and is horrified: his potential self is powerful, but he's a brute, a monster.

Then of course there is Dorian Gray,[13] he of the magic picture. Because the artist who painted the picture put too much of something or other into it – himself? His repressed passion for Dorian? – the picture is partly alive. It takes on the effects of age and experience, while Dorian (a golden boy, and related to the ancient, pagan Greeks, as his first name suggests) is freed from the consequences of his own cruel and depraved actions, remains young and beautiful, and is able to sin and collect *objets d'art* as much as he likes. He isn't an artist or a writer – nothing so banal. His *life* is the work of art, and a decadent one at that. But when he finally decides to be good and to destroy the picture, doom falls. He can't maintain his vow of virtue; realizing that the picture is his conscience, he sticks a knife into the canvas, the picture is restored to youth, and Dorian perishes. He and the uncanny picture have changed places, and Dorian now looks like what he really is – a degenerate old man. Motto: if you've got a magic picture, don't mess around with it. Leave it alone.

There's another story I would add to this collection – a strangely terrifying piece called 'The Beast with Five Fingers.'[14] At least I found it strangely terrifying when I read it as a teenager, at night, while baby-sitting. It belongs to a group which, if we were ethnographers, we might term 'The Double as Cut-OffBody-Part.' We might note, for instance, the penises coaxed away from their owners by witches and lodged in birds' nests, in that supreme metafiction, the *Malleus Maleficarum*;[15] or Gogol's story 'The Nose,' in which a man's nose runs away and becomes a court functionary in full uniform until it is trapped and reattached. 'The Beast with Five Fingers' is less amusing. A baddish nephew visits his saintly but sickly old uncle, hoping for something in the will, and notices that although the old man is asleep, his hand is not. It is busily writing – practicing, among other things, the old man's signature. The nephew considers this an interesting example of automatic writing, and thinks no more of it.

Imagine his shock when the old man dies and he receives a package containing the hand – it has forged the will, and directed that it be cut off and mailed. It is not dead at all, but leaps out and scrambles up the curtains, and begins to plague the protagonist and ruin his life, much as other doubles do. (It can write letters, for instance, and sign them with our hero's name; an inconvenient talent for such a hand.) The man traps it and nails it to a board, but it escapes, and now it has a jagged hole in it from being nailed, and is bent on revenge. Things end badly, as you might imagine: the man destroys the hand, but the hand also destroys the man, thus revealing its literary ancestry.

This hand is among other things a writing hand that has become detached from any writer. There was a Shanahan cartoon in *The New Yorker* recently that played with this idea – the Author as severed part. It shows a large finger lying in a hotel-room bed, thinking, 'Where the Hell am I?' The caption reads, 'The moving finger writes, and having writ, moves on to a three-week, twenty-city book tour.'[16] In real life it is not of course the finger who has to go on the tour, it's the luckless mortal body: that damn authorial finger, the actual perpetrator of the text, is off on its own somewhere, basking in the sun and evading the fallout.

Jorge Luis Borges went even further. In a piece called 'Borges and I' he doesn't content himself with a mere hand or single digit. Instead he takes the Jekyll and Hyde theme and applies it specifically to authorship, and splits himself – Borges – in two. 'The other one, the one called Borges, is the one things happen to,'[17] begins the half that calls himself 'I.' He goes on to tell us that Borges shares his own tastes, 'but in a vain way that turns them into the attributes of an actor. It would be an exaggeration to say that ours is a hostile relationship; I live, let myself go on living, so that Borges may contrive his literature, and this literature justifies me.' He admits that this Borges has turned out some decent enough pages, but he himself can't take credit for them. 'Besides,' he says, 'I am destined to perish, definitively, and only some instant of myself can survive in him. Little by little, I am giving over everything to him, though I am quite aware of his perverse custom of falsifying and magnifying things . . . I shall remain in Borges, not myself (if it is true that I am someone.)' The relationship may not be exactly hostile, yet it isn't friendly: 'Years ago I tried to free myself from him, and went from the mythologies of the suburbs to the games with time and infinity, but those games belong to Borges now and I shall have to imagine other things. Thus my life is a flight and I lose everything, and everything belongs to oblivion, or to him.' The writer writes himself into his work – which contains an element of posturing and artificiality – and the more he does this, the more he loses what might be called his authentic self. Yet even in setting this down, Borges is writing. He is aware of the paradox: he ends his piece by saying, 'I do not know which of us has written this page.'

This little piece sums up the self-doubts of the writer, as exemplified by the fable of the double. Can an 'author' exist, apart from the work and the name attached to it? The authorial part – the part that is out there in the world, the only part that may survive death – is not flesh and blood, not a real human being. And who is the writing 'I'? A hand must hold the pen or hit the keys, but who is in control of that hand at the moment of writing? Which half of the equation, if either, may be said to be authentic?

Now I would like to discuss some characteristics of writing as a form that might be said to have contributed to this syndrome –

the syndrome of the writer's anxiety about his other self, as well as his suspicion that he has one. It's pertinent to ask, for instance, how writing differs *as a medium* from the oral traditions that preceded it.

It has become a habit for people to speak of novelists as 'storytellers,' as in 'one of our best storytellers,' which can be a way for reviewers to get themselves off the hook – you don't have to say 'one of our best *novelists*' – and can also be a way of saying that this writer is good at plots, but not much else. Or it may be a way of indicating that the writer has a certain archaic or folkloric or outlandish or magical quality, reminiscent of a German grandmother propped in a rocking-chair telling old wives' tales, with a bunch of children and the Brothers Grimm gathered round, or of an old blind man or sharp-eyed gypsy woman sitting in the bazaar or the village square, and saying, as Robertson Davies was fond of saying, 'Give me a copper coin and I will tell you a golden tale.'[18] But there are significant differences between that sort of tale-teller beguiling his or her live audience, and the novelist in his nineteenth-century garret or study, inkwell on desk and pen in hand, or the twentieth-century one in the seedy hotel room so beloved by Cyril Connolly and Ernest Hemingway, hunched over his typewriter, or, by now, her word-processor.

Talking is very old, writing is not. Most people learn to talk when they are infants, but many people never learn to read. Reading is decoding, and in order to do it you have to learn a purely arbitrary set of markings, an abstract formula.

Not so long ago, those who could read were few. They had a rare skill, and what they did – staring at odd-shaped marks and reeling off a message written by someone far away – was regarded with awe. No wonder that, in the popular imagination, books and magic went together, and the kind of magic thought to be involved was frequently sinister. The Devil, like lawyers, was thought to go around with a contract – a big black book, which he was always pestering you to sign in blood. God, too, had his book, where the names of the saved were written, though not by themselves. Once enrolled in either book you'd be hard put to erase yourself, though it was always easier to get yourself scratched off God's good books than off the Devil's bad ones.[19]

Writing had a hardness, a permanence, that speech did not. So as soon as tale-tellers took to writing – or as soon as other people took to writing down their tales, which is more like what actually happened – the writers-down became inscribers, and what they wrote took on a fixed and unchanging quality. God doesn't content himself with speech or even with paper for the Ten Commandments: he chooses stone, thus emphasizing the solidity of what is written. Note, however, that in the New Testament, Jesus is a tale-teller. He teaches by parable, but he doesn't write a word,[20] because he himself *is* the Word, the Spirit that bloweth where it listeth; he is fluid and intangible, like the speaking voice. But among his enemies are the Scribes and Pharisees – those that hold to the letter of the law – the written-down letter. Ironic, considering that we learn about all of this out of a book. John Keats wanted as his epitaph, 'Here lies one whose name was writ in water.' How discerning of him – that way he could get the name, the writing-down of it, and also the fluidity of the Spirit, all at once.

No wonder St. Matthew looks so apprehensive in Caravaggio's painting of him, clutching his pen while a rather thuggish angel dictates to him what he must write down: the act of writing comes weighted with a burden of anxieties. The written word is so much like evidence – like something that can be used against you later. It's fitting that one of the first detective stories, that famous one by Edgar Allan Poe, featured a purloined letter.[21]

But back to the tale-teller versus the writer. There's a time-honored authorial ploy that consists of pretending to be an oral tale-teller, as Chaucer did in *The Canterbury Tales* – inventing, for good measure, a bunch of voluble folks to act as secondary tale-tellers within the tale he himself purports to be telling. And how many times have you read in some review or other that a writer has finally found his 'voice'? Of course he has done no such thing. Instead, he has found a way of writing words down in a manner that creates the *illusion* of a voice.

But deceive us how he may, a writer is not the same thing as a tale-teller. First of all, he or she is alone while composing, and the traditional tale-teller is not. The tale-teller, like the actor, must respond to an immediate audience. Her art is a performance: the instrument is the spoken voice, backed up by facial expression and gesture. This immediacy means that the tale-teller must keep within certain boundaries. Insult the audience – too much blasphemy, or more of it than the audience wants, or too much obscenity, or too many disparaging comments about the audience's native town or popular leaders or ethnic group, and so forth – and a barrage of rotten fruit or the disarticulation of your skeletal frame is likely to follow. In this way the writer of books, like the graffiti artist, is freer than the tale-teller: he doesn't stick around for feedback. Like Mary Ann Evans, the sensitive, shrinking other self of the brave and outspoken George Eliot, he can go on vacation at publication time and never even read the reviews. The reviews don't really concern him anyway – they're too late. By the time the book comes out, the text is set, the Rubicon is crossed, and the writer's job is done. Informed criticism may be of some help for the next book, but the current one, poor thing, must take its chances in the wide and wicked world.

The tale-teller in the midst of his tale can improvise, within limits – he can embroider or digress, he can add details – but he cannot revise the beginning, except between performances. Like a film seen in a theatre, his story runs one way only: you can't turn back the page and make the whole thing different. The writer, on the other hand, can scratch his way through draft after draft, laboring, like Flaubert, over the shapes of sentences, striving for exactly the right word, and throwing characters' names out the window – indeed, throwing whole characters out the window. Verbal texture and inner cohesiveness are thus arguably more important for the novelist than for the tale-teller. The best tale-tellers could improvise with language, but they often relied on standard phrases or tropes, pulled out of their word-hoard and stuck in as needed. Repetition – of words, of phrases – didn't worry them a whole lot; it's the writer, not the bard, who combs through the proofs looking for unintentional vocabulary duplications. It's not that the writer is more studied and deliberate than the tale-teller; but she is studied and deliberate in different ways.

Then there's the nature of audience. For the tale-teller, the audience is right there in front of him, but the writer's audience consists of individuals whom he may never see or know. Writer and audience are invisible to each other; the only visible thing is the book, and a reader may get hold of a book long after the writer is dead. An orally transmitted tale does not die with the teller: many such stories have been alive for thousands of years, traveling from place to place and from century to century. But the particular incarnation of the tale – that one person's way of telling it – does die. The tale thus changes from teller to teller. It is passed, not from hand to hand, but from mouth to ear to mouth. In this way it keeps moving.

A book may outlive its author, and it moves too, and it too can be said to change – but not in the manner of the telling. It changes in the manner of the reading. As many commentators

have remarked, works of literature are recreated by each generation of readers, who make them new by finding fresh meanings
in them. The printed text of a book is thus like a musical score,
which is not itself music, but becomes music when played by
musicians, or 'interpreted' by them, as we say. The act of reading
a text is like playing music and listening to it at the same time,
and the reader becomes his own interpreter.

Nevertheless, the actual, physical book gives the illusion of
permanence. (I say *the illusion*, because books can be burned
and texts lost for ever, and many have been.) A book also gives
the impression of static form, of immutability – this and no
other is the order of the words. In ages in which few could read
and texts had an aura of magic, this counted for something: witness the passage at the end of the Book of Revelation,[22] in which
the author puts a curse on anyone who might dare to change a
word of what he has set down. Under such conditions, the accu-
racy of a given text to some assumed and unique original
becomes a matter of considerable importance.

Once, texts were copied by hand; then came the age of printing, and books became infinitely replicable, thus creating the
phenomenon of multiple copies with no single authentic original. Walter Benjamin has discussed this phenomenon and its
repercussions in relation to visual art, in his essay, 'The Work of
Art in the Age of Mechanical Reproduction';[23] but it is even
more true of the book. A first manuscript version is only that –
a first version. Editings, alterations, and revisions abound, and
who is to say which version represents the writer's genuine intent?

That writer and audience may be unknown to each other
because the act of creation is separated in time from the act of
receiving it, and the infinite replicability of the book – these two
factors contributed greatly to the modern writer's equivocal view
of himself. To be a writer came to be seen as running the risk of

being the invisible half of a doubles act, and possibly also a copy for which no authentic original existed. The writer might be not only a forger, like the hand in 'The Beast with Five Fingers,' but also a forgery. An impostor. A fake.

The early-Romantic cult of the writer as a great man, a genius, the genuine article in a crowd of philistines and pinchbeck mediocrities[24] – this cult ought to have played against the images I have been discussing; that is, the doubleness of the writer, his slippery evasiveness, and his potential lack of authenticity. With improved printing and distribution methods, as well as the rapid increase in literacy, it was suddenly possible for writers to become instantly popular on a scale never before imagined, to become enormously celebrated for their work: to become larger than life, and more apparently solid than life as well. But a book that appears everywhere at once acts like a megaphone. It magnifies the voice while obliterating the human individual who gives rise to it, and the writer is obscured by the image he himself has created. Byron awoke to find himself famous, and became identified with the Byronic figure of his own poetry; but once he'd put on all that weight, it was just as well he kept out of his public's view: he could never have lived up to expectations. To be a Byronic hero is possible only in youth, even for Byron.

The Romantic genius was supposed to be one of a kind, a great original. 'Originality' in this sense (often carried to extremes, where it merged with the grotesque and the bizarre) became a touchstone, both for the public's evaluation of a writer and for the writer's evaluation of himself Chaucer and Shakespeare thought nothing of using other people's plots – in fact, to say that a story was not made up but came from an older authority, and/or had really happened, meant that it was not a frivolous lie and lent it validity. But the early Romantics held that what a man wrote was not just what oft was thought but ne'er so well expressed, and not just the well-wrought embodiment of an older myth or tale or historical event. No, it was self-expression – the expression of the self, of a man's whole being – and if a man wrote works of genius, then he had to be a genius himself, all the time. A genius while shaving, a genius while eating his lunch, a genius in poverty and in affluence, in sickness and in health – this is heavy luggage to cart around. No man is a hero to his own body, nor no woman neither. The Algonquin Indians,[25] William Burroughs,[26] and certain British cartoonists, such as Steve Bell, all have fables in which a person's rear orifice develops into an alter ego, complete with voice and personality – which is one variation on how the body subverts our more intellectual or spiritual pretensions. If you see yourself as just an honest craftsperson, you can wipe your nose on your sleeve and no one will find it out of place, but Romantic heroes and heroines, and geniuses, have – in this respect – less freedom.

So if you'd bought the Romantic-genius package – or its later version, the high-art aesthete, for whom life itself had to be a beautiful composition – you might well have felt a pressing need for a double: someone to play the more exalted part while you were snoring with your mouth open. Or, vice versa, someone to do the snoring while you were writing the poem. "'A great poet, a really great poet, is the most unpoetical of all creatures,'" says Lord Henry Wotton in *The Picture of Dorian Gray*, puncturing the early-Romantic great-poet idea by taking it to its logical conclusion – the logical conclusion being that if poetry is self-expression and a great poet puts the good stuff in himself into his work, there's not much of him left over for his life. "'Inferior poets are absolutely fascinating . . .'" says Lord Henry. "'The mere fact of having published a second-rate book of sonnets makes a man quite irresistible. He lives the poetry that he cannot write. The others write the poetry that they dare not realize."[27]

Here is one last tale about doubles. It's a science-fiction fantasy – I read it in youth, I've lost the author's name, but I'm searching – and it goes like this. A man living in a rooming-house spies on another roomer – a dowdy young woman – and learns that she is an alien, and that every evening when she comes home from work she takes off all her clothes, lies down on the floor, and attaches the top of her head to the head of a thin, flat, person-shaped skin. Then she empties herself into the skin, which fills up with her substance like a water balloon. The former empty skin is now the woman, and the newly emptied skin is rolled up and stored away. And so it goes, turn and turn about, until the voyeur can't refrain from meddling. While the woman is out he takes away the skin, and watches to see what will happen. The woman comes back and sees that her second skin is missing. She can then do nothing but wait, in quiet despair. Shortly she bursts into flames and burns to a crisp. She too cannot live without her double.

Thus the Author; capital A, and the person whose double he or she is. They alternate. They are attached head to head. Each empties his or her vital substance into the other. Neither can exist alone. To paraphrase Isak Dinesen, who said the same thing of life and death, man and woman, rich and poor, the Author and its attached human being are 'two locked caskets, of which each contains the key to the other.'[28]

I would like to conclude this chapter by re-posing Borges's dilemma: 'I do not know which of us has written this page.' According to Borges, the completed text belongs to the 'author' part of the equation – in other words, to the name without any body except a body of work – and the life out of which the text is supposedly made belongs to the mortal part of this dynamic duo.

We suspect that they both have a hand in the writing of the page – but if so, when and where? What is the nature of the crucial moment – the moment in which the writing takes place? If we could ever catch them in the act, we might have a clearer answer. But we never can. Even if we are writers ourselves, it is very hard for us to watch ourselves in mid-write, as it were: our attention must be focused then on what we are doing, not on ourselves.

Occasionally, however, a writer will try. Here is the wonderful Italian writer Primo Levi, who was also a chemist, at the end of his book called *The Periodic Table*. He has been talking about a carbon atom, and this is what he says:

> . . . I will tell just one more story, the most secret, and I will tell it with the humility and restraint of him who knows from the start that his theme is desperate, his means feeble, and the trade of clothing facts in words is bound by its very nature to fail.
>
> It is again among us, in a glass of milk. It is inserted in a very complex, long chain, yet such that almost all of its links are acceptable to the human body. It is swallowed; and since every living structure harbors a savage distrust toward every contribution of any material of living origin, the chain is meticulously broken apart and the fragments, one by one, are accepted or rejected. One, the one that concerns us, crosses the intestinal threshold and enters the bloodstream: it migrates, knocks at the door of a nerve cell, enters, and supplants the carbon which was part of it. This cell belongs to a brain, and it is my brain, the brain of the *me* who is writing; and the cell in question, and within it the atom in question, is in charge of my writing, in a gigantic minuscule game which nobody has yet described. It is that which at this instant, issuing out of a labyrinthine tangle of yeses and nos, makes my hand run along a certain path on the paper, mark it with these volutes that are signs: a double snap, up and down,

> between two levels of energy, guides this hand of mine to impress on the paper this dot, here, this one.[29]

An atom in motion. Something invisible, but common, but miraculous. We believe in it, sort of, but what we believe in more is the immediacy of Primo Levi's hand, because he uses the present tense, which means that we are right here with him while reading, and look – here is the dot his hand has just made: the period at the end of *The Periodic Table*. Still, the writer behind the hand conceived of as a bit of chemistry, the writer as carbon atom – it is somehow too bloodless for us, after all.

And so I turn to *Alice Through the Looking Glass*, always so useful in matters of the construction of alternate worlds. At the beginning of the story, Alice is on one side of the mirror – the 'life' side, if you like – and the anti-Alice, her reflection and reverse double, is on the other, or 'art' side. Like the Lady of Shalott, Alice is a mirror-gazer: the 'life' side is looking in, the 'art' side is looking out. But instead of breaking her mirror and thus discarding the 'art' side for the hard and bright 'life' side, where the 'art' side is doomed to die, Alice goes the other way. She goes *through* the mirror, and then there is only one Alice, or only one that we can follow. Instead of destroying her double, the 'real' Alice merges with the other Alice – the imagined Alice, the dream Alice, the Alice who exists nowhere. And when the 'life' side of Alice returns to the waking world, she brings the story of the mirror world back with her, and starts telling it to the cat. Which at least solves the problem of audience.

It is a false analogy, of course, because Alice is not the writer of the story about her. Nevertheless, here is my best guess, about writers and their elusive doubles, and the question of who does what as far as the actual writing goes. The act of writing takes place at the moment when Alice passes through the mirror. At this one instant, the glass barrier between the doubles dissolves, and Alice is neither here nor there, neither art nor life, neither the one thing nor the other, though at the same time she is all of these at once. At that moment time itself stops, and also stretches out, and both writer and reader have all the time not in the world.

3

Dedication:
The Great God Pen

Apollo vs. Mammon: at whose altar should the writer worship?

Nothing is truly beautiful unless it cannot be used for anything; everything that is useful is ugly because it is the expression of some need, and those of man are ignoble and disgusting, like his poor and infirm nature.
> Théophile Gautier, *Mademoiselle de Maupin*[1]

All that I am hangs by a thread tonight
As I wait for her whom no one can command.
Whatever I cherish most – youth, freedom, glory –
Fades before her who bears the flute in her hand.

And look! She comes . . . she tosses back her veil,
Staring me down, serene and pitiless.
'Are you the one,' I ask, 'whom Dante heard dictate
The lines of his Inferno?' She answers: 'Yes.'
> Anna Akhmatova, "The Muse"[2]

. . . They tore you to pieces at last, in a frenzy,
while your sound lingered on in lions and rocks,
and in trees and birds. You still sing there.

Oh you lost god! You everlasting trace! Only
Because that hatred ripped and scattered you
Are we listeners now, and one mouth of Nature.
> Rilke, *Sonnets to Orpheus*, I, 26[3]

And so rapturously, too, does he sing of his griefs, this
poet, while the dull muttonheads pick their teeth and
mount their females. Miserable clown! Can one think of
anything more ludicrous? ironic? zany? . . . Will the Poet,
as a type, join the Priest, the Warrior, the Hero, and the
Saint as melancholy museum pieces for the titillation of a
universal babbitry?

Irving Layton, Foreword, *A Red Carpet for the Sun*[4]

'I refer to the mercenary muse whom I led to the altar of
literature. Don't, my boy, put your nose into that yoke!
The awful jade will lead you a life!'

Henry James, 'The Lesson of the Master'[5]

Long ago, we are told, images were worshiped as gods, and were thought to have the powers of gods; so were certain words – the holy names. Then images became representations of gods – icons, sacred in what they pointed to, not sacred as what they were in themselves. Then they became allegorical – the images alluded to or figured forth a set of ideas or relationships or entities not presented as themselves, but by stand-ins, as it were. Then art shifted its attention, and became descriptive of the natural world, a world in which God was not visible as such but was inferred as the original fabricator, thought to be lurking somewhere in the past or behind the Newtonian scenery. Then even this assumption faded. A landscape was a landscape, a cow was a cow: they might point toward states of mind and feeling, but the mind and feeling were human. The divine Real Presence had withdrawn.

But in the West, as religion lost helium in society at large, the Real Presence crept back into the realm of art. Throughout the nineteenth century, the perception of the artist's role shifted: by the end of it, he or she was to serve this mystic entity – Art with a capital A – by assisting in the creation of sacred space, as contained within the borders of the work of art itself. When he spoke of making a new religion and building a church filled with examples from the poetic tradition, Yeats was not alone, he was simply exemplary. The sacred space of art was conceived of as either purer or more monstrous than the norm, but certainly distinct from the vulgar, money-grubbing, banal, and profane life of society at large. The artist was to be its priest, bringing Real Presence into being as the Roman Catholic priest was thought to bring the Real Presence of God into present time and place in the celebration of the Mass. Heady stuff.

There was a corollary. One mark of a true priest is his lack of interest in money: so goes the tradition, or rather the traditions, for many cultures share this view. But in a society that increasingly has come to value little else where does that leave the artist and his sacred work, not to mention his heating bill?

In the last chapter I spoke about the writer's perception that he or she is two: one that does the living and consequently the dying, the other that does the writing and becomes a name, divorced from the body but attached to the body of work. Now I would like to explore a different dichotomy – that between art and money. Put more simply, this – to use a North American colloquialism – is where the rubber meets the road. This is where the writer finds herself squeezed between the rock of artistry and the hard place of having to pay the rent. Should a writer write for money? And if not for money, then for what? What intentions are valid, what motivations pass muster? Where to draw the line between artistic integrity and net worth? To what, or to whom, should the writer's efforts be dedicated?

Already you may be thinking it's perhaps a little vulgar of me to have brought this up – this money business. I'm thinking it myself, since, for my generation – penny-pinchers though we were – talking about money was right down there with talking about your dirty laundry. But times have changed, and dirty laundry is now a salable commodity or else an installation in a cutting-edge gallery, so although you may be thinking this is vulgar, you may also be thinking it's direct and honest – indeed, almost respectable – for isn't money now the measure of all things?

In Elmore Leonard's deconstructing-Hollywood thriller *Get Shorty*, a movie star and an agent are discussing a writer, considered by both of them to be a pretty low form of pond life. "'A writer can spend years working on a book he isn't sure will ever sell. What makes him do it?'" says the movie star. "'Money. The idea of hitting it big,'" says the agent.[6] The money explanation has at least the virtue of being democratic – everyone can understand it – and also plausible, whereas any shufflings and ramblings about Art, capital A – such as those to which I will shortly subject you – would have had an antiquated and phony air in the light of Hollywood's uncomplicated and shining materialism.

Nor is this true just of Hollywood. Don't publishers leak the news of large advance sums in the hope that readers will then respect the book more? Why pretend people aren't interested? And the further away from the university classroom they get, the more interested they may admit to being. Back in 1972, I did a one-person poetry-reading tour the length of the Ottawa River Valley. This was then a somewhat remote area and not thickly strewn with bookstores; I went by bus, carted my own books with me to sell – I was good at making change, having once worked at a sports-equipment fair – and at one stage I hauled these books around behind me on a toboggan, due to a flash blizzard. In the four small towns I visited, I was the first poet to appear within living memory, or possibly ever. The readings were packed, not because people loved either poetry or me, but because they'd already seen that week's movie. The two best questions I got asked were, 'Is your hair really like that or do you get it done?' and 'How much money do you make?' Neither of these were hostile questions. Both were pertinent.

The hair question was aimed at discovering – or so I felt – whether my wild and disheveled, dare I say inspired or slightly crazed look – the right look, as everyone suspected, for a female poet – was natural to me or had been manufactured. As for the money question, this was simply an acknowledgment of my humanity: the writer has a body, which includes a stomach. Writers too must eat. You can have money of your own; you can marry money; you can attract a patron – whether a king, a duke, or an arts board; you can have a day job; or you can sell to the market. These are the choices, for a writer, in relation to money, and they are the only choices.

The money factor is often underplayed in biographies of writers, the biographer being as a rule much more fascinated by love affairs, neuroses, addictions, influences, diseases, and bad habits generally. Yet money is often definitive, not just in what a writer eats but in what he or she writes. Certain tales are emblematic – poor Walter Scott, for instance, who signed a promissory note for a partner, and upon the latter's bankruptcy scribbled himself to death to pay off the debt. Such nightmares haunt our waking moments, let alone our sleeping ones. Chained to the desk. Forced to crank out the literary fretwork, regardless of inclination, regardless of whether it's any good. Slave of the pen. What purgatory.

Even if we avoid signing promissory notes, there are many pitfalls. There is, for instance, the publishing system, and its growing domination by the bottom-line bean-counters. 'We don't sell books,' one publisher said, 'we sell solutions to marketing problems.' We've all heard the story about the writer whose first novel hasn't done well, and who then presents the second one. 'If only this were a *first* novel,' sighs the agent. 'Then I might be able to sell it.' Moral: a publisher will gamble, but –

increasingly – only once. Gone are the days – when were those days, anyway? – when a Maxwell Perkins-like publisher[7] might support a writer through two or three or four financial failures, waiting for the big breakthrough. Nowadays,

> He who writes, and makes it pay,
> Will live to write another day.[8]

If you absolutely insist on eating, and can neither sell your next novel nor get a job as a waitperson, there are literary grants, should you be able to elbow aside the thousands of others in the queue. There are creative-writing teaching posts, but there's a queue for those as well. For the newly or the effectively published, there are also international writers' festivals; there are the dreaded twenty-city book tours; there are interviews in newspapers. There didn't use to be any of those things.

Failing all of that, there is hackwork. There's publishing yourself on the Internet. And, as a last resort, there are pseudonyms. That way you can make your novel *look* like a first novel, even if it isn't one. It's a jungle out there in alphabet-land. No, it's more like a machine. It's cog eat cog.

When I found I was a writer at the age of sixteen, money was the last thing on my mind, but it shortly became the first. As I turned seventeen and eighteen and nineteen and took stock of the situation, the anxiety increased. How was I was going to live? I was brought up by my Depression-hardened parents to be, as they say now, fiscally responsible, and was expected to support myself. I had no doubt that I could do so, one way or another; but I didn't know what danger I was in as a young person attempting to live in the world as a writer, where so many forces might conspire to snuff out my light.

I didn't encounter any writing about writers and their writing lives until I'd made it to university and had run headlong into Cyril Connolly's *Enemies of Promise*, originally published in 1938 but reissued in time for me to be frightened by it.[9] It lists the very many bad things that can happen to a writer to keep him – *him* is assumed – from producing his best work. These include not only the practice of journalism – a bloodsucker for sure – but also popular success, getting too involved with political agendas, not having any money, and being a homosexual. About the most effective thing a writer could do to support himself, said Cyril Connolly – both he and I were living then in the age before the proliferation of grants – was to marry a rich woman. There wasn't much hope of this for me, but all other avenues, according to Connolly, were fraught with peril.

I did not for an instant think I would be able to make any money from writing – or not from the kind of writing I saw myself as doing. But then, selling out to the marketplace wasn't much of a threat to me at that time. For one thing, much of what I was writing was poetry. Enough said. As far as the rest of it went – by *the rest of it* I mean novels – as I've mentioned, everyone enters the scene at a certain point in time and also in a certain place, and this was Canada in the late 1950s. Everything has changed now, of course, and in my country a six-figure advance is within reach of the favored young novelist; but such things were out of the question then. There were few local publishers, and those few made their living from acting as agents for imported work, and from selling school texts. They weren't inclined to take risks, since there wasn't much demand for indigenous writing. The colonial mentality was still in force, meaning that the Great Good Place for the arts was thought to be somewhere else, such as London, Paris, or New York, and if you were a Canadian writer you were assumed by your countryfolk to be not only inferior, but pitiable, pathetic, and pretentious. Wyndham Lewis, who sat out the war in Toronto, was asked by a local matron where he was living, and when he told her, she said, 'Mr. Lewis, that is not a very fashionable address.' 'Madam,' replied the writer, '*Toronto* is not a very fashionable address.' Nor was it at the time I began writing. If you wanted to be a serious writer, you had to do it for art's sake, because there was faint hope of being able to do it for money.

By the time I was twenty I knew some people who wrote, but not one of them expected to make a living at it. To get even a crumb fallen from the literary moveable feast, you'd have to publish outside the country, and that meant you would have to write something that might snare you a foreign publisher. It went without saying that these foreign publishers were not much interested in Canada. Voltaire's dismissal of the place – '*quelques arpents de neige*' – was still the consensus. James Joyce's well-known triple-barreled slogan, 'silence, exile, and cunning,'[10] had a distinct resonance for aspiring Canadian writers, especially the exile part of it.

Thus my generation was doomed, *faute de mieux*, to a devotion to art for its own sake, though we had by no means explored the history and the iconography of that position. If we had, we might have thought that our remoteness from the temptations of Mammon was good for us: there were those who held that money, although necessary for life, was a necessary evil, at least for an artist. Starve in a garret, get some visions. However, to stay alive, one had to have at least a bit of loot – best if it was inherited, because then one didn't have to grub around for it and demean oneself; but to write *for* money, or even to be thought to have done so, put you in the prostitute category.

So it remains in certain quarters to this day. I can still hear the sneer in the tone of the Parisian intellectual who asked me, 'Is it true you write the *bestsellers?* ' 'Not on purpose,' I replied somewhat coyly. Also somewhat defensively, for I knew these equations as well as he did, and was thoroughly acquainted with both kinds of snobbery: that which ascribes value to a book because it makes lots of money, and that which ascribes value to a book because it doesn't. For the young writer who has purist ambitions, who wants to be authentic, who wants to be an artist of some sort, it's a Catch-22, especially when society in general shares the view expressed in the Eudora Welty story, 'The Petrified Man' – '"If you're so smart, why ain't you rich?"'[11] Either poor and real, or rich and a sell-out with a price-tag on your soul. So goes the mythology.

In fact, as Lewis Hyde has so definitively pointed out in his book *The Gift: Imagination and the Erotic Life of Property*,[12] any equation that tries to connect literary value and money is juggling apples and oranges. Chekhov began his career by writing exclusively for money, and never for any other reason, in order to support his poverty-stricken family. Does that make him ignoble? Shakespeare wrote for the stage, much of the time, and naturally he cranked out stuff he thought would appeal to his audience. Once he got his start, Charles Dickens tossed his day job and lived by the pen. Jane Austen and Emily Brontë didn't, though they wouldn't have minded some extra cash. But you can't say any one of these is a better or a worse artist simply because of the money factor.

Nevertheless, as Hyde points out, the part of any poem or novel that makes it a work of art doesn't derive its value from the realm of market exchange. It comes from the realm of gift, which has altogether different modes of operating. A gift is not weighed and measured, nor can it be bought. It can't be expected or demanded; rather it is granted, or else not. In theological terms it's a grace, proceeding from the fullness of being. One can pray for it, but one's prayer will not therefore be answered. If this were not so, there would never be any writer's block. The composition of a novel may be one part inspiration and nine parts perspiration, but that one part inspiration is essential if the work is to live as art. (The parts vary for poetry, but both are still involved.)

There are four ways of arranging literary worth and money: good books that make money; bad books that make money; good books that don't make money; bad books that don't make money. Those are the only four combinations. All are possible.

Again according to Hyde, the serious artist would be well advised to acquire an agent who can mediate between the realm of art and that of money; this saves the writer from any undignified and contaminating haggling on his own behalf. He may thus remain modestly apart, single in intent and pure in heart, while others with more mercenary talents bid him up and knock him down, behind closed doors.

Lacking such protection, he will have to maintain a very firm division in his own soul. It is a case of rendering unto Caesar what is his, and then paying your respects to the other one – or the other ones – who are in charge of non-Caesarly artistic affairs. One half keeps the accounts, the other worships at the shrine. Here is the useful Isak Dinesen, in a story called 'Tempests,' describing a wily old actor and theatrical producer:

> Herr Soerenson in his nature had a kind of duplicity which might . . . even be called demoniacal, but with which he himself managed to exist on harmonious terms. He was on the one hand a wide-awake, shrewd and untiring businessman, with eyes at the back of his head, a fine nose for profit, and a completely matter-of-fact and detached outlook . . . And he was at one and

the same time his art's obedient servant, a humble old
priest in the temple, with the words 'Domine, non sum
dignus' graven in his heart . . . Herr Soerenson at times
had been characterized . . . as a shameless speculator.
But in his relations to the immortals he was chaste as a
virgin.[13]

I would like to draw your attention to two suggestive phrases
here. 'A humble old priest in the temple'; and, "'*Domine, non
sum dignus.*'"[14] The temple of what, we may ask? Who is the
Lord being addressed? Herr Soerenson does not sacrifice his art to
Mammon; but who is the god he serves as a humble old priest?
We strongly suspect that it isn't Jesus.

The ease with which Isak Dinesen was able to make use of
such loaded language is the result of a long, hard battle, fought
back and forth over the intellectual and aesthetic and spiritual
high ground of the nineteenth century, and some very swampy
low ground as well. She herself had been an art student in Paris
in the first decade of the twentieth century, and would have been
more than familiar with the issues at stake in this war. The con-
testants were those who wanted art to have some worthy agenda
outside itself – to have a religious aim, or at least a moral purpose, or a socially redeeming agenda, or at the very least an
uplifting intent, or at the very, very least, an optimistic and
healthy-minded and cheerful effect – and, in the other corner,
those who proclaimed the self-sufficiency of art and its exemp-
tion from any need for social justification whatsoever. This war is
by no means over; it breaks out anew every time there's a fight
over some piece of public funding for, say, an art show that might
include pee in a bottle or a dead cow or a picture of a Moors
Murderer. So, since what any sort of artist – writers included –
actually does is influenced in part by what he thinks he's supposed to be doing, and what on the other hand he thinks he's

prohibited from doing, it's as well to run briefly over a few past features of the fray.

At the outset of this war, it was only established religion that was in the habit of claiming a more or less total freedom from external judgment: it reserved the right to dole out the moral standards and not be subjected to any, apart from those con- cocted by itself. Were the champions of art for art, then, aspiring to the status of a religion? In a word, yes. And couldn't that be considered blasphemous? Yes, again. To be a poet, in the middle of this war, meant you might have to be a *poète maudit*, doomed to Hell but defiant, like Mozart's Don Giovanni, who achieved a cult status in the nineteenth century of a kind he never had in the eighteenth. Or like Byron. Or like Baudelaire. Or like Rimbaud. Or like Swinburne. And so forth.

There was a certain nobility in such damnation: you were true to your position, however reprehensible that position might be, even though it might land you in Hell itself. There might even be a higher truth involved: the Victorians were fond of higher truths, so if you were going into battle it was just as well to have a higher truth on your side. The reason- ing, had it been spelled out, might have gone something like this:

'The truth shall make you free,'[15] said Jesus. 'Beauty is Truth, Truth, Beauty,'[16] said John Keats. By the rules of the syllogism, if truth is beauty and the truth shall make you free, then beauty shall make you free, and since we are in favor of freedom, or have been off and on since it was extolled in the Romantic age, we should devote ourselves to beauty-worship. And where is beauty – widely interpreted – more manifest than in Art? This train of thought pursued to its end leads to the conclusion that even the aesthetic turning away from the moral dimension had, itself, a moral dimension. And if the pursuit of perfect artistic expression is not the sole aim of the artist, what other aims might he or she legitimately be expected to have?[17]

Tennyson set himself this problem early on in his career, in a somewhat programmatic poem called 'The Palace of Art.'[18]

> I built my soul a lordly pleasure-house,
>   Wherein at ease for aye to dwell.
> I said, 'O Soul, make merry and carouse,
>   Dear soul, for all is well.'

So it begins. There follows an interior-decoration catalog of *objets d'art* worthy of Dorian Gray or of any of Henry James's dubious aesthetes; but it turns out not to be enough. The Palace of Art is a lovely building, with many well-wrought urns and golden fountains and Greek statues and other inspiring doo-dads in it, but the soul can't live there. To do so would be too isolated and thus selfish, and also too sterile; in addition, the soul has made a god of Art, and is thus guilty of idolatry. "'I sit as God holding no form of creed,'" she says, "'but contemplating all.'" Thus she is guilty of 'serpent pride,' the worst sin, and shortly falls into a deep despair.

As an artist – especially as an artist – the poet's soul has to go where the human action is, and for Tennyson that always means a descent from the heights, because love – whether for one person or for humanity – is of the valley. The Palace of Art isn't repudiated and destroyed in this poem, but it has to be human-ized.

> So when four years were wholly finished,
>   She threw her royal robes away.
> 'Make me a cottage in the vale,' she said,
>   'Where I may mourn and pray.

'Yet pull not down my palace towers, that are
    So lightly, beautifully built;
Perchance I may return with others there
    When I have purged my guilt.'[19]

Once you've got down and dirty and done some suffering and atonement, maybe you can move back in, and bring other folks with you, thus turning the Palace of Art into – well, the National Gallery, perhaps.

The artistic insights of one age become the clichés of the next. I remember two popular songs from the fifties, one of which urged me to come down from my ivory tower and let love come into my heart, and another in which the woman is addressed as Mona Lisa, and asked whether she is warm and real, or just a cold and lonely, lovely work of art. Art is cold, life is warm, goes this formulation: a reverse of the situation in Keats's Grecian urn in the eponymous Ode, in which time is frozen and the rapescene-in-progress depicted on it is arrested at its hottest moment, and it is the human observers who will grow old and cold. (This Grecian urn, with its alive–dead, cold–hot reverses, is *The Picture of Dorian Gray*[20] in the making.)

The nineteenth-century battle over the proper function of art was fierce, but all attempts to bend art to some useful purpose, or to prove that it had such a purpose – even attempts by the likes of art-lovers such as Ruskin and Matthew Arnold – came to grief in the end, because what they amounted to was censorship. If beauty is truth and the truth will make you free, is there a kind of truth that ought to be suppressed? Yes: ugly truth, or any truth that might be bad for you, which is why John Ruskin destroyed many of Turner's erotic drawings. Those who preached the social usefulness of art wanted the warts covered up, much as the Pope had covered up the dangly bits on Michelangelo's Sistine Chapel during the Counter-Reformation.

It wasn't only sex that needed to be expurgated: it might be rabble-rousing political ideas, or critical notions about religion, or undue violence and squalor, and so forth. Still, most often it was sex, and novelists of the time knew quite well that there were some things they couldn't write for general publication, because such things simply would not be printed. Thus the heroes of Art became those who were willing, as they say now, to push the envelope.

Some writers pushed the envelope too far and came into overt conflict with the authorities. 'Flaubert,' says Borges, 'was the first to consecrate himself (and I use the word in its full etymological rigour) to the creation of a purely aesthetic work in prose.'[21] Flaubert is thus another priest in the temple – a self-consecrated priest at that – who dedicated himself to the purely aesthetic, and was thus a natural suspect in the war between art and moral purpose. He was put on trial for *Madame Bovary*, and found himself in the unpleasant position of having to play by his enemies' rules – that is, to demonstrate that his book had a healthy moral. He defended it by claiming that the moral was healthy because Madame Bovary died a gruesome death as the result of her adulteries. (Strictly considered, untrue – if she hadn't foolishly overspent, she would have got away with it.)

The censors and the Mrs. Grundys were busy bees for many decades, their efforts culminating in such triumphs as the banning of James Joyce's *Ulysses*, but the hypocrisy demanded by the pillars of society fueled the revolt of the artists. Taken to its extreme, this gave us Henry Miller and William Burroughs: it wasn't a case of dreaming the impossible dream, but of printing the unprintable word. The scrum went on for a long time. When I was an undergraduate, *Lady Chatterley's Lover* still hadn't passed its court test in Canada, and Henry Miller's *Tropic of Cancer* had to be smuggled into the country.

To put all of this in context: you could not then – in the late fifties – buy contraceptives over the counter, and you couldn't buy them at all if you were an unmarried woman; you could not get an abortion except somewhere else, or on a kitchen table; the first time I read Hemingway's story 'Hills Like White Elephants,' I had no idea what the man and the woman were discussing. You could not advertise sanitary products for women and call them what they were, which gave rise to a degree of surrealism unmatched in advertising since. I remember in particular a woman in a white Grecian-style evening gown standing on a marble staircase and gazing out over the sea, with a caption under her that said, 'Modess . . . Because.' *Because what*? I wondered as a child. This is a question that still recurs in dreams.

But back to the art wars. 'Art for art,' the strange device on the banner[22] raised by Théophile Gautier – in defiance of the social good, of the improvement of the individual, of moral earnestness, and so forth – this device was the credo that finally prevailed among the devotees of Art. Toward the end of the century, Oscar Wilde could proclaim, without being any more shocking than he intended to be,

> The moral life of man forms part of the subject-matter of the artist . . . No artist has ethical sympathies. An ethical sympathy in an artist is an unpardonable mannerism of style. No artist is ever morbid. Vice and virtue are to the artist instruments of an art . . . The only excuse for making a useless thing is that one admires it intensely. All art is quite useless.[23]

What then of the kinds of people who were to make these use-less but admirable things – admirable in their own right, since 'beauty is its own excuse for being,'[24] said Emerson, just like

God? 'The artist is the creator of beautiful things,' says Wilde.
'To reveal art and conceal the artist is art's aim.'[25] Far from being
the self-expressing Romantic genius, the artist is now to be self-
effacing; he is to be hidden from view, and he is to serve his
calling. James Joyce's already cited trio, 'silence, exile, and cunning,' argues an asceticism and a self-denial worthy of a
Dominican monk in training. The writer-as-artist is to be,
according to Joyce, a 'priest of the imagination.'[26]

Art is an abstract category. A priest, however, implies a god: you
can't have one without the other. If Art is to be a god, or to have a
god, then what sort of god? There's one answer in the poem 'A
Musical Instrument,' written in 1860 by Elizabeth Barrett
Browning, in the midst of the war I've been describing, but before
the scales had tipped definitively in favor of art for art. Here it is:

> I
> What was he doing, the great god Pan,
> Down in the reeds by the river?
> Spreading ruin and scattering ban,
> Splashing and paddling with hoofs of a goat,
> And breaking the golden lilies afloat
> With the dragon-fly on the river.
>
> II
> He tore out a reed, the great god Pan,
> From the deep cool bed of the river;
> The limpid water turbidly ran,
> And the broken lilies a-dying lay,
> And the dragon-fly had fled away,
> Ere he brought it out of the river.
>
> III
> High on the shore sat the great god Pan
> While turbidly flowed the river;
> And hacked and hewed as a great god can,

With his hard bleak steel at the patient reed,
Till there was not a sign of the leaf indeed
To prove it fresh from the river.

IV
He cut it short, did the great god Pan
(How tall it stood in the river!),
Then drew the pith, like the heart of a man,
Steadily from the outside ring,
And notched the poor dry empty thing
In holes, as he sat by the river.

V
'This is the way,' laughed the great god Pan
(Laughed while he sat by the river),
'The only way, since gods began
To make sweet music, they could succeed.'
Then, dropping his mouth to a hole in the reed,
He blew in power by the river.

VI
Sweet, sweet, sweet, O Pan!
Piercing sweet by the river!
Blinding sweet, O great god Pan!
The sun on the hill forgot to die,
And the lilies revived, and the dragon-fly
Came back to dream on the river.

VII
Yet half a beast is the great god Pan,
To laugh as he sits by the river,
Making a poet out of a man;
The true gods sigh for the cost and pain –
For the reed which grows nevermore again
As a reed with the reeds in the river.[27]

Or, as D. H. Lawrence later put it, 'Not I, not I, but the wind that blows through me.'²⁸ Or, as Rilke says in his third Sonnet to Orpheus,

> . . . song is existence. Easy for the god. But
> when do *we* exist? And when does he spend
>
> the earth and the stars on our being?
> When we love? That's what you think when
>   you're young;
> not so, though your voice forces open your mouth, –
> learn to forget how you sang. That fades.
> Real singing is a different kind of breath.
> A nothing-breath. A ripple in the god. A wind.²⁹

In Barrett Browning's poem, the poet is an instrument for the making of music, and it is beautiful music. But the poet doesn't make the music of his own volition. First, he is chosen by the god. He is set apart from the rest of his fellows, and can never rejoin them. Second, he is mutilated. His heart is taken out of him, and he becomes hollow, dry, and empty. He can make music only through inspiration – the god blows through him. Not only that, the god isn't a very nice god: Pan is half a beast – the bottom half. The Great God Pan cares only for the music, not at all for the poet whom he has hollowed out, and who will – we assume – be cruelly cast aside as a broken reed when the god is finished with him. There are other gods in the poem – the 'true gods,' who care about the cost and pain; but we suspect they are lousy musicians. In Art, you don't get aesthetic points for good intentions. The pagan God of Art may be a nasty piece of work, and an idol too – a false god – but you can't say he isn't good at what he does. So if it's art you crave – beautiful art – love him or hate him, this is the god you must pray to.

This version of the God of Art – a cruel and selfish god – may seem to smack of high-Victorian moralism, but it underlies even the most fervent aestheticism of the late nineteenth and early twentieth centuries. The God of High Art – just as in Barrett Browning's poem – requires human sacrifices. If Art is a religion and artists are its priests, it follows that artists too must sacrifice. What they must sacrifice is the more human parts of themselves – the heart first. They must sacrifice the possibility of human love, like priests, in order to more perfectly serve their god.

'Those who find beautiful meanings in beautiful things are the cultivated,' says Oscar Wilde, defending his own book. 'For these there is hope. They are the elect to whom beautiful things mean only Beauty.'[30] This is the language of Christianity – hope being the hope of salvation, and 'the elect' being those predestined for it. A small band of initiates, then; a select few, a saving remnant.

But among the elect, martyrdom is always a possibility; and to be an artist is not altogether a choice – the God of Art picks you, not the other way around. Therefore the artistic vocation has an aura of tragedy and doom about it. 'We poets in our youth begin in gladness,' said Wordsworth, 'But thereof comes in the end despondency and madness.'[31] Consider Franz Kafka's story, 'A Fasting-Artist.' The fasting-artist is an artist dedicated completely to his art. This art is grotesque: the artist stays in a cage and starves himself – much like a self-mortifying Christian ascetic of old – and at first he is very popular: crowds flock to marvel at him. Then fashions change – the art-for-art's sake fashion was by Kafka's time falling out of widespread favor – and the fasting-artist ends up in a neglected corner of a circus menagerie, and people forget he's in the cage. Finally they poke around in the rotten straw and rediscover him, more dead than alive. Here's what happens next:

'I always wanted you to admire my fasting,' said the
fasting-artist. 'And we do admire it,' said the overseer
obligingly. 'But you shouldn't admire it,' the fasting-artist
said. 'All right, we don't admire it then,' said the overseer,
'but why shouldn't we admire it?' 'Because I have to fast,
I can't help it,' said the fasting-artist. 'Whatever next,'
said the overseer. 'And why can't you help it?' 'Because,'
said the fasting-artist . . . 'I could never find the
nourishment I liked. Had I found it, believe me, I would
never have caused any stir, and would have eaten my fill
just like you and everyone else.' Those were his last
words . . .[32]

The fasting-artist's hunger, like that of the saints, is for a food
not of this world; in this he is sublime. But he is also ridiculous,
because he is such a dingy misfit. The God of Art has chosen the
fasting-artist as his disciple, but the Kafkaesque result is a combination side-show freak and Freudian compulsive.

Once you start counting the bodies – the bodies at the foot of
the altar of Art – they are numerous. By the time of George
Gissing's 1891 novel, *New Grub Street*, writers had come to view
themselves and their activities as fitting subjects for their own art,
thus giving rise to the huge – and growing – number of books in
which writers write about writers writing. In *New Grub Street*,
there are three main writers. The first is caddish Jasper Milvain,
an out-and-out worshiper of Mammon who's in the literary game
for money and has no aspirations to be a priest of the imagination. He says he's not 'cut out for the work' of novels – 'It's a pity,
of course – there's a great deal of money in it.'[33] He prospers, as
the wicked often do in this world. The second is Edwin Reardon
who has talent and sensitivity and high principles, and marries a
socially conscious woman on the strength of a modest literary
success. But under the pressure of his wife's expectations of
money, inspiration deserts him, and he suffers one of the most

agonizing attacks of writer's block ever described. When he can't produce, his wife leaves him; then he gets ill and dies. The third writer is poor Harold Biffen, who has toiled away, Flaubert-like, at a slice of realism called *Mr. Bailey, Grocer*. This novel is a failure — 'A pretentious book of the *genre ennuyant*,'[34] say the reviewers — but Biffen opts for the a-man-can-but-do-his-best *Ivanhoe* defence. 'The work was done — the best he was capable of — and this satisfied him.' Finally, having run out of both hope and money, he chooses suicide. His death is peaceful — 'Only thoughts of beautiful things came into his mind; he had reverted to an earlier period of life, when as yet no mission of literary realism had been imposed upon him . . .'[35] Ah, that fateful imposed mission. Many are called, but few are chosen, and among those few, some will be martyred.

If sacrifice was demanded of the male artist, how much more so of the women? What leads us to suspect that the fancifully embroidered scarlet letter on the breast of the punished and reviled Hester Prynne, in Hawthorne's novel of the same name, stands not only for Adulteress, but for Artist, or even Author? A man playing the role of Great Artist was expected to Live Life — this chore was part of his consecration to his art — and Living Life meant, among other things wine, women, and song. But if a female writer tried the wine and the men, she was likely to be considered a slut and a drunk, so she was stuck with the song; and better still if it was a swan song. Ordinary women were supposed to get married, but not women artists. A male artist could have marriage and children on the side, as long as he didn't let them get in the way — a faint hope, according to James, Connolly *et al.* — but for women, such things were supposed to *be* the way. And so this particular way must be renounced altogether by the female artist, in order to clear the way for that other way — the way of Art.

Thus Malli, the young actress who is to play Ariel to Herr Soerenson's Prospero in his production of *The Tempest*, in the Isak Dinesen story already mentioned. In great distress, Malli gives up her passionate human love for her art. "'What do we get in return?'" she then quite reasonably asks Herr Soerenson. "'In return,'" he says, "'we get the world's distrust – and our dire loneliness. And nothing else.'"[36]

That's bleak, but it can get bleaker. Thus the young actress Sibyl Vane in *Dorian Gray* – what chance has she got, with a name like that?[37] Like the Lady of Shalott – Ophelia's younger sister, and the singing-and-dying prototype for female artists in the nineteenth century, whom Sibyl dutifully quotes – she falls in love with a flesh-and-blood man, and because she is now putting her emotion into her life and not into her art, the God of Art punishes her, and her talent deserts her. 'Without your art you are nothing,' says Dorian, deserting her in his turn. What can poor hollow, dry, empty, broken-reed Sibyl do after that but commit suicide?

When she had herself photographed lying in her own coffin, the actress Sarah Bernhardt knew exactly what she was doing. The necrophilia and black drapery played well, because this was the image of a woman artist the public wanted and could understand: a sort of half-dead nun.

When I was an aspiring female poet, in the late 1950s, the notion of required sacrifice was simply accepted. The same was true for any sort of career for a woman, but Art was worse, because the sacrifice required was more complete. You couldn't be a wife and mother and also an artist, because each one of these things required total dedication. As nine-year-olds we'd all been trotted off to see the film *The Red Shoes* as a birthday-party treat: we remembered Moira Shearer, torn between Art and love, squashing herself under a train. Love and marriage pulled one way, Art another, and Art was a kind of demonic possession. Art would dance you to death. It would move in and take you over, and then destroy you. Or it would destroy you as an ordinary woman.

But you didn't have to be a nun of the imagination or nothing. The feminine of *priest* is not only *nun* but *priestess*, so you had a choice, and there was a difference: the Christian religion had no priestesses, so there was something pagan and possibly orgiastic implicit in the term. Nuns were cut off from men, priestesses weren't, though their relations with men were not usually what you would call domestic.

I first ran into the priestesses of Art in Robert Graves's book, *The White Goddess*,[38] in which it is maintained that women can't be real poets unless they take on the role of the Nightmare Life-in-Death Triple Goddess, and, as her priestesses, crush men underfoot like bugs and drink their blood like wine.[39] I read this when I was nineteen or so, and it was not encouraging to a girl who had been runner-up in the Consumers' Gas Miss Homemaker Contest: drinking the blood of my paramours was not my idea of a fun-time Saturday-night date. Provincial of me, but there you are. Graves did shake me up, though, and cause me to wonder whether I was really cut out for the life of Art.

I wondered even more when I ran across George Eliot's 1876 novel *Daniel Deronda*. The hero's mother has been a great opera singer, and has passed Daniel into other hands at the age of two, partly because she doesn't want motherhood getting in her artistic way. She's had lots of admirers, but having been dominated by her father she is a cold fish, and prefers men prone, with her foot on their necks. She claims she's not a monster, but the language describing her gives us pause. She is 'not quite a human mother, but a "Melusina'" – half woman, half snake.[40]

'Looking at her,' says Eliot, Daniel feels 'the sort of commotion that might have been excited if he had seen her going through some strange rite of a religion that gave a sacredness to crime.'[41] We can make a good guess as to what that religion is, especially when we are told that she has put all of her emotions into her art, and has 'nothing to give.'[42] She remains partly human in that she suffers, but the largest amount of her suffering is connected with her abandonment of her art, not with the abandonment of her child. Giving up her singing is a sin against her religion – the religion of Art – and she has been punished for it.

Daniel's mother is also called a sorceress, and it's a short step from that to the *femme fatale*, dozens of which species litter the scene by the end of the nineteenth century. One of the favorite figures of this era was Salomé, whose name I learned early as a skipping rhyme: *Salomey was a dancer, she did the hootchie kootch, And when she did the hoochie kootch, she didn't wear very mooch.* On the artistic level, we have Flaubert's 'Salomé' (the short story), Oscar Wilde's *Salomé* (the play), Richard Strauss's *Salomé* (the opera), and many a painting. It is to her that T. S. Eliot's J. Alfred Prufrock refers when he envisages his own head being borne in upon a platter. What was the appeal? Salomé is a figure in whom the fatal woman and the female artist are combined. She's very good at her art, good enough to seduce most viewers, but she allows this art to be corrupted by the promise of reward, first by Herod, who promises her anything she wants in return for her dancing, and then, in some versions, by her erotic passion for John the Baptist: if she can't have all of him, she'll take at least the head. Finally – in Wilde and Strauss, at least – she is crushed to death for being so perverse, or else for taking off the seventh veil – we're never entirely sure.

Oddly enough, a remarkable number of the poems submitted by young women to the college literary magazine I helped to edit in 1960 were about Salomé. The fear seemed to be that your involvement with art would prove fatal to any man hapless enough to cross your sexual path, and you'd wake up one morning to find his head on a plate. It's a vaguely Freudian position, I suppose: women who are too active or too smart cause men to shed their body parts at the drop of a veil.

This was the decade just after Phillip Wylie's *Generation of Vipers* had placed the blame for all the ills of the world on 'Momism,' which in turn continued the nineteenth-century tradition – still very much alive then – of worrying about the castrating female. Here is Irving Layton, in the Foreword to his 1958 collection, *A Red Carpet for the Sun*:

> Modern women I see cast in the role of furies striving to castrate the male; their efforts aided by all the malignant forces of a civilization that has rendered the male's creative role of revelation superfluous – if not an industrial hazard and a nuisance. We're being feminized and proletarianized at one and the same time. This is the inglorious age of the mass-woman. Her tastes are dominant everywhere . . . Dionysus is dead . . .[43]

A strange brew for me to encounter at the age of eighteen, while striving to be a poet. From this distance I can spot the mixed metaphors – the Furies usually went after men for the sin of matricide, and the Maenads, those frantic dismemberers of men and of Orpheus the poet, were not the slayers of Dionysus but his worshipers; though this fact did not make the male poets of the day feel any safer from women and their supposed lust for gonad-snipping.

And sometimes female writers allied themselves with this

mythology. If you've got the name, you might as well join the game. Both the nun of the imagination and the priestess of the imagination may finish up in a non-living condition at the foot of Art's altar, but the difference is that the priestess takes someone else with her when she goes. 'I eat men like air,' says death-defying, death-embracing Lady Lazarus, with her sorceress's long red hair, in Sylvia Plath's poem of that name – thus placing herself firmly in this tradition.

The drawbacks to being a female writer – especially a female poet – were well known by the time I got there. Germaine Greer, in her very thorough book *Slip-Shod Sibyls*,[44] has recounted the sad careers and frequently grim deaths of female poets from the late eighteenth to the mid-twentieth centuries. Emily Dickinson and her reclusiveness, Christina Rossetti looking at life through the worm-holes in a shroud, Elizabeth Barrett Browning and her drug-addiction and anorexia, Charlotte Mew, a suicide, Sylvia Plath, another suicide, Anne Sexton, yet another. 'The blood jet is poetry,' wrote Sylvia Plath, ten days before her own suicide. 'There is no stopping it.'[45] Is that where the priestess of the imagination was fated to end up – as a red puddle on the floor?

The doomed female artist is far from dead, especially as a theme for novelists to explore. A. S. Byatt's novel *Possession* rings complex changes on this figure – the female poet who renounces human love – and so, even more wickedly, does Carol Shields's novel *Swann* – a female poet dedicated to her art and murdered by her husband because he can't stand the competition. However, one of these novels is set in the past and another in a remote rural area. Unless you make your female artist a self-destructive, drug-raddled, promiscuous, hugely famous rock-singer, as in Salman Rushdie's latest novel *The Ground Beneath Her Feet*, it's not as easy today to play this image of the dying swan as fully contemporary, and, also absolutely straight, the way it was once played.

However, it was still being played straight enough when I was starting to write. So much a part of the job description did it appear that after my first two slim volumes had been published I was asked, in all honesty, not whether I was going to commit suicide, but when. Unless you were willing to put your life on the line – or rather, dispose of it altogether – you would not be taken quite seriously as a woman poet. Or so the mythology decreed. Luckily I wrote fiction as well as poetry. Though there are some suicidal novelists too, I did feel that prose had a balancing effect. More meat and potatoes on the plate, you could say, and fewer cut-off heads.

Now it is more possible for a woman writer to be seen as, well, just that: neither nun nor orgiastic priestess, neither more nor less than human. Nevertheless, the mythology still has power, because such mythologies about women still have power. Maenad and Pythoness wait in the wings, or their empty costumes do, and nothing is more likely to call them back again than the cult of art for art.

In the first chapter, I spoke about the fact that various expectations and anxieties are projected onto the role of the Writer, capital W. In this chapter I touched on one batch of these – the ones having to do with the rejection of the worldly values of Mammon in favor of a total dedication to Art, and with the notions of sacrifice that came to be associated with this dedication.

But what happens when you avoid the Slough of Despond on the 'narrow is the road and strait is the gate' path of Art-for-Art's Sake, and take another path – the one signposted Social Relevance?[46] Will you end up on a panel discussion, and if so, is it the panel discussion in Hell? But if you turn your back on Social Relevance, won't you end up making the equivalent of verbal doilies for the gilded armchairs in the Palace of Art? It's always a possibility.

4

Temptation:
Prospero, the Wizard of Oz, Mephisto & Co.

Who waves the wand, pulls the strings, or signs the Devil's book?

Again, the devil taketh him up into an exceeding high mountain, and sheweth him all the kingdoms of the world, and the glory of them;

And saith unto him, All these things will I give thee if thou wilt fall down and worship me.

Matthew 4: 8–9

One must be possessed of the Devil to succeed in any of the arts.

Voltaire[1]

This court jester is expensive!

Frederick the Great, of Voltaire[2]

I hope you will not ask me what it all means, or what the moral of it is. I rank myself with the historian in this business of tale-telling, and consider that my sole affair is to hunt the argument dispassionately. Your romancer must . . . affect a genial height, that of a jigger of strings; and his attitude should be that of the Pulpiteer . . .

Maurice Hewlett, *The Forest Lovers*[3]

. . . the poet must not be a poet, he must be some sort of moral quack doctor.

Edith Sitwell[4]

. . . if we look at writers through the ages we see that they
have always been political . . . To deny politics to a writer
is to deny him part of his humanity.
     Cyril Connolly, *Enemies of Promise*[5]

Some, patagonian in their own esteem,
and longing for the multiplying word,
join party and wear pins, now have a message,
an ear, and the convention-hall's regard.
Upon the knees of ventriloquists, they own,
of their dandled brightness, only the paint and board.
     A. M. Klein, 'Portrait of the Poet as Landscape'[6]

A shame he couldn't manipulate natural elements as he
could manipulate human logic and belief . . . If success
did not come, the magic-maker could sigh for the plight
of the human race, its loss of mystical dignity and his loss
of money; if success came, the magic-maker could take it
with delicacy and restraint, keeping a good eye on
practicalities. Or he could double under the weight of his
people's devotion if he were an unusually sincere
magician with super-respect for his craft. And fear for its
real power.
     Gwendolyn MacEwen, *Julian the Magician*[7]

In the last chapter I said that images were once gods, but the corollary of that is that gods were once images. We know of god-images that appeared to eat, others that appeared to speak, and yet others with furnaces inside them in which children were sacrificed. Artificers made the images, priests acted as the puppeteers behind the scenes.

The images themselves – those graven images of the sort denounced and derided by the Old Testament prophets – were cold, hard, and inert; yet they were of considerable fascination to the art-for-art writers in the second half of the nineteenth century. They were works of art; they might also be semi-animate idols, like the Vénus de l'Isle that crushes her beloved to death in Mérimée's eponymous story, or like the death-dealing goddess in Flaubert's brutal and much-bedizened *Salammbô*. Underneath the raging conflict between the producers of art and its potential consumers was a subtext that had to do with idolatry. Is the worship of 'false' gods – including the false gods of Art and Beauty, when split off from the needs of human society – not merely neutral, but the worship of evil? How guilty – therefore – should a writer feel about his art?

No writer appears to have felt more anxiety in the face of such questions than Henry James. In 1909, he published *The Lesson of the Master*, in which were collected a number of stories written primarily in the 1890s for *The Yellow Book*. This was the magazine of the Aesthetic Movement, of which he fundamentally disapproved. Each of these stories is about a writer, or writers: an older writer who urges a younger one to adopt a selfless, priestly dedication to his art, along with sexual abstinence, and then marries the desired girl himself; a wonderful, obscure writer who is discovered and 'lionized' by a social world that doesn't understand his art, an experience which kills him; a poor, authentic writer who vainly longs for money and recognition, while a rich, famous, vulgar one – a woman – vainly longs instead for the artistic cachet that comes with popular failure; a master writer, the central secret of whose art no one can quite make out; and a writer who has a brilliant reputation, but is, underneath it all, a fraud. James had nervous fun with these stories, and taken together they demarcate the essentially Flaubertian attitudes toward 'being a writer' which had coalesced into received writerly wisdom by that time.

There is another story that might well have been included in this gallery: 'The Author of *Beltraffio*,' first published in 1884. But this tale is altogether darker. A writer called Marc Ambient – Marc for Marcus Aurelius, possibly, and Ambient as in *ambient glow*, perhaps – this master writer has produced a masterwork, a novel called *Beltraffio*, which is a kind of 'aesthetic warcry.' He lives in a charming 'palace of art, on a slightly reduced scale,' and has a lovely little son; but he is married to a 'narrow, cold, Calvinistic wife, a rigid moralist,' who despises his love of beauty and thinks his books are evil – so much so that she tries to keep her son away from his father, and dreads the day when he will be old enough to read Ambient's work, thus becoming corrupted by it. Of her, it is sneeringly said that she believes art should have a '"purpose."' Among those who ascribe to the 'gospel of art,' what heresy!

On the surface of things, the perfection-seeking Ambient might seem to be the 'good' embodiment of James's own artistic views, with the wife incarnating nasty constipated philistinism. But that is just on the surface: Henry James had too much of the American Puritan in him to be an amoral aesthete. Marc Ambient considers 'all life' to be 'plastic material' for his art, and that art is of a suspicious nature. He says of it,

> 'This new affair must be a golden vessel, filled with the purest distillation of the actual; and oh how it worries me, the shaping of the vase, the hammering of the metal! I have to hammer it so fine, so smooth . . . And all the while I have to be so careful not to let a drop of the liquor escape!'[8]

The Grecian urn again, perhaps, but in a context that suggests not only the sort of Daedalus-like craftsman–artificer invoked at the end of Joyce's *Portrait of the Artist as a Young Man*, but also the alchemist, dabbler in distillations. And what sort of vessel is he making with such toil, and what does it hold? The elixir of life, or the blood of a sacrifice?

The latter, we suspect by the end of the story; for husband–artist and wife–society manage to kill their child between them. That the wife does not bear the sole responsibility – that the child is sacrificed not just to the mean, cramped idol of conventional morality, but also to the gilded idol of Art – is suggested by the name of Ambient's masterwork. 'Beltraffio' is not a real word, and does not appear to be a place name, Italian or otherwise; but it is worth mentioning that 'tra' in Italian means 'among,' while 'fio' means 'penalty.' As for 'bel,' it is 'beautiful,' of course; but *Belzebù* is the Italian word for *Beelzebub,* the Devil – cognate with all the Bels and Baals of the ancient Middle East, so frequently anathematized in the Bible. At the end of her life, we are told, the wife dips into 'the black "Beltraffio."' We can only hope her soul survived the reading, for, in the Western literary tradition, a black book can have only one owner.

As for the child, he might have been saved by a compromise between art and society; but what form might such a compromise have taken? This is certainly a question that kept James awake nights.

In the last chapter I spoke about the often drastic mythologies concerning the writer as artist, a self-dedicated priest or priestess of the imagination, serving the exacting, demanding, and potentially destructive cult of art for art's sake. If a writer places himself within this framework, then he will see his duty as devotion to his art, and his desired goal as the creation of a perfect work. In truth, if you do not acknowledge at least some loyalty to this ideal, as the musician Klesmer tells the society girl Gwendolen Harleth in George Eliot's novel *Daniel Deronda*, you are unlikely to achieve more than mediocrity, and perhaps a 'glaring insignificance.'[9] An art of any kind is a discipline; not only a craft – that too – but a discipline in the religious sense, in which the vigil of waiting, the creation of a receptive spiritual emptiness, and the denial of self all play their part.

But that is to consider the artist only in relation to his art. What about his relation to the outside world – to what we call society? Large claims have been made in this respect. The pen is mightier than the sword,[10] we are told; the poet is the unacknowledged legislator of the world.[11]

This may be overdoing it a bit, especially in the age of the atom bomb, the Internet, and the rapid disappearance of other species from this earth. But still, let us suppose that the words the writer writes do not exist in some walled garden called 'literature,' but actually get out there into the world, and have effects and consequences. Don't we then have to begin talking about ethics and responsibilities, and other, similarly irksome things that the priest of the imagination has claimed it as his prerogative to disregard?

But let us think again about the word *priest*. Isn't a priest more than a worshiper, one who serves in a ritual sense? Isn't he also a shepherd of the people, a mediator between God and everybody else? Joyce's Stephen Dedalus sets out to 'forge in the smithy of my soul the uncreated conscience of my race.'[12] *Conscience*: that's a morally loaded word. If the writer has such powers, let us consider the wielding of these powers, both in relation to the wielders – the writers – and to the wieldees – the rest of us.

Nobody hates writers more than writers do. The most vicious and contemptuous portraits of writers, both as individuals and as types, appear in books written by writers themselves. Nobody loves them more, either. Megalomania and paranoia share the writer's mirror. The writer-as-Faust looks into it and sees a grandiose and evil and superhuman Mephistopheles, master of magic, controller of destinies, to whom other human beings are as puppets whose strings he controls, or as fools whose hearts and deepest secrets he holds in the palm of his hand; the writer-as-Mephistopheles looks into the same mirror and sees a shivering and pathetic Faust, longing for eternal youth and terrific sex and untold riches, and clutching desperately to the pitifully delusional belief that he can conjure up these things through the miserable scribbling, the puerile fooling around with words, that he has the overweening nerve to call 'art.'

In the twentieth century, writers have on the whole been haunted by the specter of their own inconsequence. Not Shelley's powerful world-shaping poet, but Eliot's hesitant J. Alfred Prufrock, has been the general pattern. Books about the loathsomeness or enviousness or pettiness or foolishness of the writer proliferate. Here is a portrait of the writer as messed-up geek, from Don De Lillo's *Mao II*. An editor is describing his work, to a writer:

> 'For many happy years, I've listened to writers and their brilliant kvetching. The most successful writers make the biggest complainers . . . I wonder if the qualities that produce the top writer also account for the ingenuity and size of his complaints. Does writing come out of bitterness and rage or does it produce bitterness and rage? . . . The solitude is killing. The nights are sleepless. The days are taut with worry and pain. Bemoan, bemoan . . .'
>
> 'It must be hard for you,' [says the writer], 'dealing with these wretches day after day.'
>
> 'No, it's easy. I take them to a major eatery. I say, Pooh pooh pooh pooh. I say, Drinky drinky drinky. I tell them their books are doing splendidly in the chains. I tell them readers are flocking to the malls. I say, Coochy coochy coo . . . There is miniseries interest, there is audio-cassette interest, the White House wants a copy for the den.'[13]

And here, from a short story by Mavis Gallant called 'A Painful Affair,' is a letter from English writer Prism to French writer Grippes, explaining why Grippes should not come to live in London, as he has suggested he may do:

> In Paris, Prism wrote, Grippes could be recognized on sight as a literary odd-jobs man with style. No one would call him a climber – at least, not to his face. Rather, Grippes seemed to have been dropped in early youth into one of those middling-high peaks of Paris bohemia from which the artist can see both machine-knit and cashmere blazers hanging in the Boulevard Haussmann department stores and five-thousand-franc custom tailoring. In

England, where caste signs were radically different, he
might give the false impression that he was a procurer or
a drug pusher and be gunned down at a bus stop.[14]

Prism and Grippes are both vain, both highly sensitive about
their own reputations; each tries to do the other down over the
most trivial of imagined slights. Martin Amis's novel *The
Information* is similar, as are many, many more, among the most
recent being – for instance – the 'writer' characters in David
Foster Wallace's *Brief Interviews With Hideous Men*. Why this
self-loathing? Perhaps it's the gap between the image – inherited
from the Romantics – and the reality. What will the glorious
dead, the giants of literature, make of their ninety-pound-weak-
ling descendants?

Here is A. M. Klein on the modern poet's ignominious obscurity:

We are sure only that from our real society
he has disappeared; he simply does not count,
except in the pullulation of vital statistics –
somebody's vote, perhaps, an anonymous taunt
of the Gallup poll, a dot in a government table –
but not felt, and certainly far from eminent –
in a shouting mob, somebody's sigh.

O, he who unrolled our culture from his scroll –
the prince's quote, the rostrum-sounding roar –
who under one name made articulate
heaven, and under another the seven-circled air,
is, if he is at all, a number, an x,
a Mr. Smith in a hotel register, –
incognito, lost, lacunal.[15]

(This psychic wound appears to be suffered largely by men.
Women writers weren't included in the Romantic roll-call, and

never had a lot of Genius medals stuck onto them; in fact, the word 'genius' and the word 'woman' just don't really fit together in our language, because the kind of eccentricity expected of male 'geniuses' would simply result in the label 'crazy,' should it be practiced by a woman. 'Talented,' 'great,' even – these words have been applied. But even when they really did affect their own societies, female artists have not often confessed to the ambition to do so. Consequently those of the present day don't feel a slippage in their power or a demotion in their place on the world's stage, and they may suspect that they're doing better today than previously, so they don't feel too puny by comparison with a horde of illustrious female ancestors.)

I will now attempt to discuss some of the alternatives to the high-minded art-for-art identity of the writer, and the crises of self-perception such alternative identities may involve. One of these concerns the curious node where art and money and power intersect; the other – and it is not unrelated – concerns something we refer to as 'moral responsibility,' or else as 'social responsibility.' The place where others touch the artist – in ways that might control what is produced – we could label 'money and power.' The place where the artist touches others through what he produces we could label 'moral and social responsibility.'

The money-and-power question can be boiled down to its shortest form: is your soul on the market, and if so what's the price, and who's the buyer, and who will crush you like a soft-shelled crab if you don't sell, and what do you hope to get in return?

Here is a joke:

> The Devil comes to the writer and says, 'I will make you the best writer of your generation. Never mind

generation – of this century. No – this millennium! Not
only the best, but the most famous, and also the richest;
in addition to that, you will be very influential and your
glory will endure for ever. All you have to do is sell me
your grandmother, your mother, your wife, your kids,
your dog and your soul.'

   'Sure,' says the writer, 'Absolutely – give me the pen,
where do I sign?' Then he hesitates. 'Just a minute,' he
says. 'What's the catch?'

Suppose the writer signs the Devil's document, and suppose
that worldly power is part of the contract, as it would have been
for Jesus had he succumbed to the Tempter in the desert. If a
writer gets this kind of power, at what point can he be said to be
misusing it? The short form of the social responsibility problem
is probably: are you your brother's keeper, and if so to what
extent, and are you willing to mangle your artistic standards and
become a Pulpiteer, a preachy manipulator of two-dimensional
images, in order to ram home some – usually somebody else's –
worthy message or other?

And if you aren't your brother's keeper, if you stay shut within
your ivory tower, are you, by default, Cain the homicidal – no,
the fratricidal, since all men are brothers – with blood on your
hands and a mark on your forehead? Does your inaction lead to
societal crime?

There are no neat answers; but if you take up writing, you'll
run into the questions sooner or later. Perhaps I shouldn't even
call them questions. Perhaps I should call them 'conundrums.'

First, the problem of moral and social responsibility in relation to
the content of a work of art. For instance, if a man murders
someone, then he is a murderer, and will be caught if possible,
and put on trial, and so forth. But if a writer murders someone

in a book – if he has a character dedicate himself to the com-
mission of the perfect murder as an aesthetic act, a work of art, as
for instance André Gide has done in *Les Caves du Vatican* – then
what is he guilty of, and how are we to judge his crime? Should
we – indeed, can we – evaluate his book simply according to aesthetic standards, as an art-object – how mellifluous the
paragraphs, how symmetrical or lopsided the structure, whether
or not the metaphors are both apt and unusual, or whether the
plot ends with a satisfying bang or an ironic whimper? And what
if his paper murder inspires someone else to commit a real one?

Is the writer above the moral law – is he a Nietzschean *Über-
mensch,* to whom the ordinary rules observed by the boring,
dimwitted, talentless, run-of-the-mill *hoi polloi* ought not to
apply? On the other hand, if writing does not express merely
Itself-as-an-art-object – if it really is *self*-expression, on the part of
the writer – what kind of self can such a murder-creating writer
be exposing to view? Not a very nice one, you'd say. An amoral
self at best; at worst, a gloating monster.

Susan Sontag, chief priestess of both high modernism and
high postmodernism, speaking recently about her early anti-
traditional essays, delivered herself of the following confession:

> I was involved in an intense self-mortification . . . Those
> essays aren't just austere, they're positively ascetic, as if I
> didn't trust the sensuality of my imagination. I think I
> was afraid of getting lost. I just wanted to support things
> that were good and that would be improving to people,
> and that was natural to me, because I always had a
> moralistic frame of mind.[16]

Improving to people. Ah yes. Every parent longs for it, this
improving function of art, and every school board in North
America would agree with it, and some of them would then use

their agreement as an excuse for censorship. But *improving to people* how? And which people, and in what ways do they need to be improved? Improved, and also protected from influences that some might consider counter-improving?

Thereby hangs a tale, and it's a very long tale. It includes Plato wishing to kick the poets out of the ideal state proposed in the *Republic*, because of the lies they told; it includes not a few book-burnings, and some people-burnings too, and such things as fatwahs and Papal Indexes, not to mention the fact that your Aunt Lila won't speak to you because she thinks she is Madame X, the profligate floozy in your latest novel, and she never did any such thing, and how dare you. Serves you right for filching her finger-wave and her 1945 nip-waisted suit, and pasting them onto someone completely different.

But was it really your right as an artist to purloin Aunt Lila's wardrobe? Are you entitled to make off with the conversations you overhear in bus stations and stick them into some recondite construction of your own? Can everything and everyone be used by you – viewed as *material*, as they are by Hugo, the writer whose wife calls him a 'filthy moral idiot' in the Alice Munro short story called 'Material'? Hugo is the epitome of the hateful writer, and at first his wife doesn't believe he really *is* a writer:

> He did not have the authority I thought a writer should
> have. He was too nervous, too touchy with everybody,
> too much of a showoff. I believed that writers were calm,
> sad people, knowing too much. I believed that there was
> a difference about them, some hard and shining, rare
> intimidating quality they had from the beginning, and
> Hugo didn't have it.[17]

But as it turns out, Hugo does have it. After they're divorced, the wife comes across a story by Hugo, which Hugo has created

by stealing the wife's descriptions of their former downstairs
neighbor, Dotty, with whom he never had much to do in real life.
It's a very good story, says the wife:

> I am not moved by tricks. Or if I am, they have to be
> good tricks. Lovely tricks, honest tricks. There is Dotty
> lifted out of life and held in light, suspended in the
> marvellous clear jelly Hugo has spent all his life learning
> how to make. It is an act of magic, there is no getting
> around it . . . [Dotty] has passed into Art. It doesn't
> happen to everybody.[18]

The wife sits down to write a note of appreciation to Hugo, but
finds herself writing in anger: '*This is not enough, Hugo. You
think it is, but it isn't. You are mistaken.*'[19]

What isn't enough? The lovely tricks, the magic. The art. It
doesn't compensate – or not in the wife's mind – for the filthy
moral idiocy of Hugo.

Start asking what *would* be enough, and *enough* in what terms,
and a whole pile of questions come pouring out of the box.
Should the god of the artist be Apollo the Classicist, with his
beautiful formality, or Mercury, the mischief-maker, trickster,
and thief? Should you invoke as your inspiration the Holy Spirit,
as Milton did in *Paradise Lost*, or a Muse of fire, as in the
Prologue to Shakespeare's *Henry V*, or Harry Houdini, the hocus-
pocus man?

In what ways, if any, does talent set you apart? Does it exempt
you from the duties and responsibilities expected of others? Or
does it load you up with even more duties and responsibilities,
but of a different kind? Are you to be a detached observer, pur-
suing your art for its own sake, and having arcane kinds of fun –
or rather, experiences that will enrich your understanding of Life

and the Human Condition – and if you do this to the exclusion of other people and their needs, will you become your own sin-soaked gargoyle? Or ought you to be a dedicated spokesperson for the downtrodden of this earth, like Gogol or Charles Dickens or Victor Hugo or the Zola of *Germinal* or the Orwell of *Down and Out in Paris and London*? Should you write your own *J'accuse,* like Zola, or are all such accusations vulgar? Ought you to support worthy causes, or avoid them like the plague? Are you, *vis-à-vis* the average taxpayer, a superfluous parasite, or the essential heart of the matter? Should you be tagged as some dreary 'intellectual worker,' as in various Communist regimes of yester-year – ever anxious about whether you're getting the party line right? The party line may be of any kind at all: the knots of 1930s left-wing political correctness are, as knots, much like the right-wing religiously correct knots of not so very long before that time, and not so far also from the ideological neo-liberal knots of today. In every case of party lines, reality is seen through a lens, and the lens distorts.

For instance, there's the F-word. If you're a woman and a writer, does the combination of gender and vocation automatically make you a feminist, and what does that mean, exactly? That you shouldn't put a good man into your books, even though you may in real life have managed to dig up a specimen or two? And if you do courageously admit to being one of those F-word females, how should this self-categorization influence your wardrobe choices? I know that's a frivolous comment, but if the wardrobe matter is all that frivolous, then why have so many earnest commentators made such ideological heavy work of it? And even if you aren't an F-word feminist in any strict ideological sense, will nervous critics wallop you over the head for being one, simply because you exemplify that suspicious character, A Woman Who Writes? If, that is, you put any female characters into your books who aren't happy, and any men who aren't good. Well, probably they will. It's happened before.

In short: if you acknowledge any responsibility to society at all, even insofar as you claim to describe it, does your vocation make you the master of all you survey, or the slave of somebody else's lamp?

There's 'good,' there's 'good at,' and there's 'good for,' in the sense of *good for* other people. In which of these ways should art and artists be 'good'? Many more panel discussions than I care to dwell on have been devoted to such topics; they usually have titles like 'The Writer and Society,' and assume the writer has, or ought to have, a function in relation to everybody else, and that it should be a useful rather than a merely decorative or entertaining function – decoration and entertainment being viewed by some, though not by all, as lightweight if not sinful – and that the usefulness of this function should be measurable by a yardstick other than that of artists themselves. There is never any shortage of people who can think up good things for you to do which are not the same as the things you are good at.

I want to run a mile – although I don't always manage it – when asked to participate in such discussions. No doubt this is because I was told, in 1960, as a twenty-year-old poet, by an older poet who was a man, that I would never come to anything as a poet until I had been a truck-driver, thus learning at first hand what real people actually did all day. I don't think there are any tried and true correlations of that reliable cause-and-effect sausage-machine kind between life and art, or none that have to do with quality – that is, raw material into the truck-driver's seat, and after a while, accomplished top-grade artist out the other door. But perhaps if it had been possible for me to hire myself out as a female truck-driver – which it was not, yet, there and then – I would have done it, and it would have become one of those formative experiences biographers are so fond of talking about, and then I might have thought otherwise.

'Is it necessary to suffer in order to be a writer?' aspiring writers are in the habit of asking. 'Don't worry about the suffering,' I have tended to say. 'The suffering will occur whether you like it or not.' What I ought to add is that, many times, the suffering is a *result* of the writing, rather than its cause. Why? Because there are a lot of people out there who'll be damned if they let you get away with it, you jumped-up smarty-pants. Publishing a book is often very much like being put on trial, for some offense which is quite other than the one you know in your heart you've committed. "'It's the novelist who understands the secret life, the rage that underlies all obscurity and neglect. You're half murderers, most of you,'" says a character in *Mao II*;[20] and many critics, and many outraged members of vigilante committees dedicated to cleaning up the reading material of the youth of today, and many governments of totalitarian regimes, share this view. They know there's a body buried somewhere, and they're keen to dig it up, and then to hunt you down. Trouble is, it's not usually the right body.

How does writing differ in this respect from the other arts – or, these days, *media* – if indeed it does? All come in for their share of vilification: artists of every kind have been lined up in front of the firing squads. But I'd say writers are especially prone to retaliation by those who have the power to denounce them, and to assassinate them on the street, and to drop them out of helicopters, not only because they're so mouthy, but also because – like it or not – language has a moral dimension built into it: you can't say *weed* without making a negative judgment about the botanical specimens you've just assigned to the weed category.

When I was a university student, we were all expected to be familiar with an Archibald MacLeish poem called 'Ars Poetica'

that contained the lines, 'A poem should be palpable and mute /
As a ripe fruit,' and ended, 'A poem should not mean, but be.'[21]
Of course this poem contradicted its own strictures: it was a
poem, but it was hardly mute and devoid of meaning; indeed, it
was situated firmly in the didactic tradition. Critics held for a
long time that it ought to be the aim of art both to delight and
to instruct, and I'd say this poem falls pretty heavily on the
instruction side of the fence. You might even call *it prescriptive.*
Much more so than, say, Gertrude Stein's famous little rhyme,
'Pigeons on the grass alas.'[22] Nor does the MacLeish poem resemble the Cézanne-like meditation on the essence of appleness that
it holds out as the ideal for poetry – lyric poetry, presumably, as
you can hardly expect the *Iliad* or the *Inferno* to possess nothing
but these fruit-like qualities.

I asked a recent house-guest – a novelist[23] – for her opinion.
Was it possible, I said, to write a story with no moral implications
at all? 'No,' she said. 'You can't help the moral implication,
because a story has to come out one way or the other, and the
reader will have opinions about the rightness or wrongness of the
outcome, whether you like it or not.' She recalled various authors
who had tried to do away with this element: Gide in *Lafcadio*,
Robbe-Grillet, who declared that he was out to dispose of two
obsolete concepts, character and plot. I do remember reading the
latter in the late fifties – it was sort of like reading a cafeteria tray
before you've put anything on it. That having been said, I'd also
say that Robbe-Grillet came pretty close to writing morally neutral prose. But this prose was also neutral in most other ways –
ways that make much writing of interest. 'His essays are a
scream,' said my friend. 'Yes, but do you still read his novels?' I
said. 'No,' she said. 'Nothing happens, and there aren't any jokes.'

Value judgments on the characters or the outcome need not be
made by the writer, at least not in any overt fashion. It was

Chekhov who said famously, and not quite truthfully, that he never judged his characters, and you will find many a critical review that tacitly endorses this sort of restraint. But the reader will judge the characters, because the reader will interpret. We all interpret, every day – we must interpret, not only language, but a whole environment in which *this* means *that* – 'little green man' means cross the street, 'little red man' means don't – and if we didn't interpret, we'd be dead. Language is not morally neutral because the human brain is not neutral in its desires. Neither is the dog brain. Neither is the bird brain: crows hate owls. We like some things and dislike others, we approve of some things and disapprove of others. Such is the nature of being an organism.

Where does that leave art for art's sake? Between a swinging door and a brick wall, you'd think. And that's where it is, out there in the free-for-all, never-never land of newspapers and political reactions and market forces, where art and society clash over such things as elephant-dung-ornamented Madonnas, with both sides taking the tickets and counting the cash.

'Poets are magicians without quick wrists,'[24] said Gwendolyn MacEwen. I'd like to come at this subject from a different angle now by talking about three fictional characters, all of them quasi-magicians. These are: the Wizard of Oz in the L. Frank Baum children's story of the same name, Prospero in Shakespeare's play *The Tempest*, and the power-mad actor Henrik Höfgen in Klaus Mann's novel *Mephisto*. What do all three have in common? All exist at the intersection of art with power, and therefore with moral and social responsibility. And all three are illusionists, of one kind or another, like Hugo the filthy moral idiot and his wonderful magic jelly.

First, *The Wizard of Oz* – a book I read early in life. As you know, it concerns Dorothy, a Kansas girl who is carried away by a tornado to the Land of Oz, where witches, good and evil, still exist. Dorothy sets out for the Emerald City, where everything is green and there is said to be a wizard who can facilitate her journey back to Kansas. After many adventures she gets there, along with a Cowardly Lion who believes he lacks bravery, a Scarecrow who thinks he has no brain, and a Tin Woodman who claims to be missing a heart. All are in search of personal life-enhancement and increased self-esteem, and they seek these from the Wizard, who appears to each one differently: Oz the Great and Terrible is a giant head, a raging fire, a beast, and a lovely woman.

But during Dorothy's audience, her dog Toto knocks over a screen in the corner, and the real Wizard is revealed – a little old man, who was been working the whole show with the aid of props, tricks, and ventriloquism. It is he too who has arranged, by means of colored spectacles, for the Emerald City to look so green; but he has practiced all these deceptions, he explains, for the good of his people. He's had to pretend to be magical and fearsome, so that the evil witches – who really do have supernatural powers – would not destroy them all. Thus he has created either a utopia or a benevolent despotism, however you choose to look at it. Also he has fooled Dorothy into doing battle with the remaining evil witch by holding out false promises: he doesn't really know how to get her back to Kansas.

Dorothy is not impressed. 'I think you are a very bad man,' she says.

'Oh, no, my dear,' says the Wizard. 'I'm really a very good man; but I'm a very bad Wizard . . .'[25]

If you're an *artist*, being a good man – or a good woman – is pretty much beside the point when it comes to your actual accomplishments. Moral perfection won't compensate for your badness as an artist: not being able to hit high C is not redeemed by being kind to dogs. However, whether you are a good man or a bad man is *not* beside the point if you happen to be a good *wizard* – good at doing your magic, making your 'marvellous clear jelly,' creating illusions that can convince people of their truth – because if you are good at being a wizard in this sense, then power of various sorts may well come your way – power in relation to society – and then your goodness or badness as a human being will have a part in determining what you do with this power.

The Wizard of Oz – *soi-disant* magician, wielder of power, manipulator, illusionist, and fraud – has a long genealogy. His remote ancestor was probably a shaman or high priest or con-juror, or one who combined these functions. Other ancestors can be found in folklore. More recently, and in literature, he can be traced from Marlowe's Dr. Faustus through Prospero of *The Tempest*. Prospero begot Jonson's *Alchemist*, and *The Alchemist* begot Thackeray's Prologue to *Vanity Fair* with its puppet-show world controlled by the puppeteer as author. He also begot a lot of tyrannical magicians and artist figures, including Nathaniel Hawthorne's sinister or deluded alchemists of 'The Birthmark' and 'Rappacinni's Daughter.' Sometimes things turned nasty, and we got the bad magicians of E. T. A. Hoffmann – see also the Offenbach opera, *Tales of Hoffmann*, – and George du Maurier's exploitative hypnotist Svengali in *Trilby*, and then there was some fooling around under the table, and who knows who begot whom, and further along there were the creepy shoemaker in the film *The Red Shoes,* and the master of the wax museum in Joseph Roth's novel *The Tale of the Thousand and Second Night,* who creates illusionary monsters because that's what people want. Then there are Thomas Mann's hypnotist in 'Mario and the Magician,' and Robertson Davies's master-magician Eisengrim the Great, alias Paul Dempster, in the Deptford trilogy, and Bergman's tormented hero in his film *The Magician*. They range from showmen out to make a buck to those who wish to manipulate the lives of others for fun and profit, to those who suspect their magic may in fact be real, and that the world of wonders they concoct really *is* a wonder, and a creator of wonder in others.

Let us then consider Shakespeare's Prospero, for he is in a way the grand-daddy of all the rest. We know his story. Betrayed by his usurping brother, cast away with his daughter and his books – including, not incidentally, his books of magic – he fetches up on a tropical island, where he attempts to civilize the one native available to him, the witch-born Caliban, and when this fails keeps him under control by aid of enchantment. Along come the bad brother and the King of Naples and his court, shipwrecked on the island. Prospero calls up his familiar, the airborne elemental, Ariel, and proceeds to entice, confuse, and scare the pants off those erstwhile enemies whom Fate has now put into his power. His aim is not revenge, according to him – he wants to bring about their repentance: 'They being penitent, / The sole drift of my purpose doth extend / Not a frown farther,' as he says. Once they are penitent, his own restoration as the Duke of Milan will follow, and also the marriage of his worthy daughter with the worthy son of the King, thus forestalling the proposed assassination of the latter. In short, Prospero uses his arts – magic arts, arts of illusion – not just for entertainment, though he does some of that as well, but for the purposes of moral and social improvement.

That being said, it must also be said that Prospero plays God. If you don't happen to agree with him – as Caliban doesn't – you'd call him a tyrant, as Caliban does. With just a slight twist, Prospero might be the Grand Inquisitor, torturing people for their own good. You might also call him a usurper – he's stolen the island from Caliban, just as his own brother has stolen the dukedom from him; and you might call him a sorcerer, as Caliban also terms him. We – the audience – are inclined to give him the benefit of the doubt, and to see him as a benevolent despot. Or we are inclined most of the time. But Caliban is not without insight.

Without his art, Prospero would be unable to rule. It's this that gives him his power. As Caliban points out, minus his books he's nothing. So an element of fraud is present in this magician figure, right from the beginning: altogether, he's an ambiguous gentleman. Well, of course he's ambiguous – he's an artist, after all. At the end of the play Prospero speaks the Epilogue, both in his own character and in that of the actor that plays him; and also in that of the author who has created him, yet another behind-the-scenes tyrannical controller of the action. Consider the words in which Prospero, alias the actor who plays him, alias Shakespeare who wrote his lines, begs the indulgence of the audience: 'As you from crimes would pardoned be, / Let your indulgence set me free.' It wasn't the last time that art and crime were ever equated. Prospero knows he's been up to something, and that something is a little guilt-making.

The third illusionist I promised you is the actor Henrik Höfgen, from Klaus Mann's 1936 novel *Mephisto*. Höfgen is an artist – a real artist. He's an actor, and a very good one; his best role is Mephistopheles in Goethe's *Faust*. But the novel is set during the Third Reich, and Höfgen becomes his own Mephisto; he tempts the susceptible Faust part of himself, and leads himself down the unholy road to worldly power. To get this power, he cuddles up to the Nazis, not because he believes their creed but because that's where the goodies are. He betrays his erstwhile left-wing friends, including his best pal Otto, and throws over his lover because she's black. "'The theatre needs me,'" he says, "'and the regime needs the theatre.'" How right he is – totalitarianism is always somewhat theatrical. And, like the theatre, it leans heavily on illusion: grand façades, with squalor and string-pulling behind the scenes.

Finally Höfgen is visited by a messenger – a young man bearing a message from Otto, who has just been tortured to death by the SS. The message is, roughly, *We shall overcome, and when we do, we'll know who to hang.* Höfgen is unnerved by this visit. "'What do people want from me?'" he whimpers. "'Why do they pursue me? Why are they so mean to me? I'm only a poor actor!'"[26]

When things get tough, Mephisto dumps his costume and reverts to the frightened human being behind the illusion. But does that let him off the hook for the things he's done in order to obtain his high position and his loot, with his art as both disguise and instrument?

In all such magician or wizard or illusionist figures, the question of imposture, of trickery, of manipulation for power of one kind or another, is never very far away. It seems that when the artist tries for a sphere of power beyond that of his art, he's on shifty ground; but if he doesn't engage himself with the social world at all, he risks being simply irrelevant – a doodler, a fabricator of scrimshaw, a fiddler with bric-à-brac, a recluse who spends his time figuring out how many angels can prance on the head of a pen.

What to do? Where to turn? How to proceed? Is there a self-identity for the writer that combines responsibility with artistic integrity? If there is, what might it be? Ask the age we live in, and it might reply – the witness. And, if possible, the eyewitness.

It's an old role, this. *I was there, I saw it, it happened to me*: these are seductive recommendations, and make a deep appeal to the imagination, as writers from Herodotus on have known. 'Good prose is like a window-pane,'[27] says George Orwell, implying that what we see through this clear window will be the truth, the whole truth, and nothing but the truth.

'I only am escaped alone to tell thee,' say the four messengers in the Book of Job.[28] Someone has to survive in order to tell what happened, an old man says to the starving violinist portrayed by Vanessa Redgrave in the concentration-camp film *Playing for Time*, as he hands her his own bit of sausage. Captivity narratives, castaway narratives, war stories, civil-war stories, slavery narratives, catastrophe stories, memoirs of hard-done-by outlaws and pirates, incest-survivor stories, Soviet Union gulag stories, atrocity stories: how much more compelling we find them if we think they're based on real events, and especially real events that have happened to the writer!

The power of such narratives is immense, especially when combined with artistic power. And the courage required to write them, and sometimes to smuggle them across borders so they can be published, is equally stupendous. These stories exist in a realm that is neither fact nor fiction, but perhaps both: let us call it enhanced fact. To mention two supreme examples of this form – the Polish writer Ryszard Kapuscinski's book *The Emperor*, about the fall of the Emperor of Ethiopia; and Curzio Malaparte's astonishing book *Kaputt*, written secretly by him, in fragments, behind the Nazi lines in World War II – a book for which he would certainly have been shot, had any of its pages been found in his possession.

Real life's jagged extremes mixed with verbal artistry are a potent and sometimes explosive combination. This is why so many people have faked such stories, beginning at least with

Daniel Defoe. Some have even concocted false identities in order to do so. Fake North American Indians, fake Australian indigenous people, fake Holocaust survivors, fake mistreated women, even fake Ukrainians – over the years, the totals have added up, and these are only the ones who've been found out. Even when an eyewitness story isn't forged, but is a piece of fiction and admitted to be such, writers can be accused of appropriating the voices of others. A socially conscious writer can quite easily be charged with exploiting the misery and misfortune of the downtrodden for his own gain. Does that put *Oliver Twist* in a new light? Is Charles Dickens a social reformer and upholder of virtue and justice, or a filthy moral idiot, like Alice Munro's Hugo? The line between these is sometimes thin, and sometimes it's only in the eye of the beholder.

Then, too, the eyewitness can be a kind of voyeur. In Leon Edel's introduction to Henry James's 1901 novel *The Sacred Fount*, Edel reports a review of that time as saying that James's novel gave 'the effect of a man peeping through a keyhole at a man peeping through a keyhole.'[29] The protagonist of that novel is, not incidentally, a novelist; but the joke is that although he's always spying on people, he isn't sure in the end exactly what he has really seen. The Henri Barbusse novel *L'Enfer* takes place in a hotel room, from which vantage point the narrator looks through a peephole at the gritty goings-on in the next room. This is quite a distance from those favorite eighteenth-century onlooking personae, the idler and the spectator, and a distance too from our familiar twentieth-century friends, 'angle of vision' and 'point of view,' but they're in the same club – there's the one who looks, namely the writer, and those who are looked at. Thus the huge pair of spectacles that dominates the scene in *The Great Gatsby* – a leftover ad for an oculist, but functioning in the book like the eyes of an amoral and indeed powerless God – seeing everything, doing nothing, with vacancy in place of a head. *Eyes Without A Face*, proclaimed the title of one of the first modern poetry collections I ever read.[30]

I Am A Camera, stated the title of the well-known Christopher Isherwood book. Actually, nobody is a camera, so where did this particular self-definition come from? From the same place the private eye came from, we suspect: that particular blend of aestheticism and science that produced, toward the end of the nineteenth century, both Sherlock Holmes, the dope-taking, violin-playing, eagle-eyed snoop, and Oscar Wilde's Lord Henry Wotton, the supreme aesthete, detached observer, and chemist-like experimenter with other people's emotional lives.

What did Yeats mean when he told a future generation of poets to cast a cold eye on life and death? Why does the eye have to be so cold? That bothered me for years. Perhaps Yeats was throwing in his lot, finally, decisively, on the side of craft, on art as artifice, as opposed to the political involvement that had occupied him earlier in his day. Or perhaps he meant something like this, from Brian Moore's 1962 novel, *An Answer from Limbo*. The protagonist, a writer, stands at his mother's graveside:

> Above the pit, their shovels moving as one, the
> gravediggers dug, filled; dug, filled. Earth fell on earth . . .
> The priest shut his prayer book. Remember this.
>   And then, as though he had come up beside me, that
> drunken, revengeful Brendan . . . repeated in my ear his
> angry words at Dortmunder's party: STANDING BY HIS
> WIFE'S BEDSIDE WATCHING HER FACE CONTORT, THE BETTER
> TO RECORD HER DEATH AGONY. HE CAN'T HELP DOING IT.
> HE'S A WRITER. HE CAN'T FEEL: HE CAN ONLY RECORD.

"'I have altered beyond all self-recognition,'" thinks the writer. "'I have lost and sacrificed myself.'"[31]

So here we are again, with the cold-eyed, cold-hearted artist, the one who has sacrificed himself for his art and forfeited his human ability to feel, but this time there's a distinct suggestion of a pact with the devil. Not only the heart has gone, but the soul has been lost as well.

There can be, however, another reason for the coldness of the artist's eye. Consider the ending of Adrienne Rich's poem, 'From the Prison House':

> This eye
> is not for weeping
> its vision
>   must be unblurred
> though tears are on my face
>
> its intent is clarity
>   it must forget
> nothing[32]

This is the eye of the scribe of the Egyptian and Mesopotamian Underworlds, or of the recording angel of the Christian Heaven. The eye is cold because it is clear, and it is clear because its owner must look: he must look at everything. Then she must record.

How is the writer to determine his or her position in relation to the rest of humanity? Where on the ladder of power should he take his place, if indeed such a place is even on offer any more? How to choose? As I've said, I have no answers. But I've indicated some of the possibilities, some of the dangers that may lurk; some of the conundrums. As for advice, should you be a young writer – I could say, as Alice Munro has said, 'Do what you want and live with the consequences.' Or I could say, 'Go where the story takes you.' Or I could say, 'Take care of the writing, and the social relevance will take care of itself.'

And this in fact is true, because the secret is – and you are welcome to use it at any panel discussion you may find yourself serving on – the secret is that it isn't the writer who decides whether or not his work is relevant. Instead it's the reader. And it is to the reader that we will turn our attention in the next chapter.

5

Communion:
Nobody to Nobody
The eternal triangle: the writer, the reader, and the book as go-between

How pleased therefore will the reader be to find that we have, in the following work, adhered closely to one of the highest principles of the best cook which the present age, or perhaps that of Heliogabulus, hath produced . . . By this means, we doubt not but our reader may be rendered desirous to read on for ever, as the great person, just above-mentioned, is supposed to have made some persons eat.

    Henry Fielding, *Tom Jones*[1]

A man listening to a story is in the company of the storyteller; even a man reading one shares this companionship. The reader of a novel, however, is isolated, more so than any other reader . . . In this solitude of his, the reader of a novel seizes upon his material more jealously than anyone else. He is ready to make it his own, to devour it, as it were.

    Walter Benjamin, 'The Storyteller'[2]

As Detlev von Liliencron wrote, his rhymes dripping with sarcasm: it is hard for the poet to evade fame. If he cannot secure the favor of the masses in his lifetime, posterity will praise his heroic way of starving to death. In a word, to sell was to sell out.

    Peter Gay, *The Pleasure Wars*[3]

. . . for we are great statements in our days and on the
basis of that we can expect small audiences.
    Gwendolyn MacEwen, 'The Choice'[4]

The big blundering newspaper had discovered him, and
now he was proclaimed and anointed and crowned. His
place was assigned to him as publicly as if a fat usher with
a wand had pointed to the topmost chair . . . In a flash,
somehow, all was different; the tremendous wave I speak
of had swept something away. It had knocked down, I
suppose, my little customary altar, my twinkling tapers
and my flowers, and had reared itself into a temple vast
and bare. When Neil Paraday should come out of the
house he would come out a contemporary. That was what
had happened: the poor man was to be squeezed into his
horrible age.
    Henry James, 'The Death of the Lion'[5]

I rip the envelope and I'm in Bangkok
. . . You pour from these squares, these blue envoys.
And just when I feel I've lost you to the world,
I can't keep up,
Your postcard comes with the words
'wait for me.'
    Anne Michaels, 'Letters from Martha'[6]

I would like to begin by talking about messengers. Messengers always exist in a triangular situation – the one who sends the message, the message-bearer, whether human or inorganic, and the one who receives the message. Picture, therefore, a triangle, but not a complete triangle: something more like an upside-down V. The writer and the reader are at the two lateral corners, but there's no line joining them. Between them – whether above or below – is a third point, which is the written word, or the text, or the book, or the poem, or the letter, or whatever you would like to call it. This third point is the only point of contact between the other two. As I used to say to my writing students in the distant days when I had some, 'Respect the page. It's all you've got.'

The writer communicates with the page. The reader also communicates with the page. The writer and the reader communicate only through the page. This is one of the syllogisms of writing as such. Pay no attention to the facsimiles of the writer that appear on talkshows, in newspaper interviews, and the like – they ought not to have anything to do with what goes on between you, the reader, and the page you are reading, where an invisible hand has previously left some marks for you to decipher, much as one of John Le Carré's dead spies has left a water-logged shoe with a small packet in it for George Smiley.[7] I know this is a far-fetched image, but it is also curiously apt, since the reader is – among other things – a sort of spy. A spy, a trespasser, someone in the habit of reading other people's letters and diaries. As Northrop Frye has implied, the reader does not hear, he overhears.[8]

So far I've spoken primarily about writers. Now it's the turn of readers, more or less. The questions I would like to pose are, first: for whom does the writer write? And, secondly: what is the book's function – or duty, if you like – in its position between writer and reader? What ought it to be doing, in the opinion of its writer? And finally, a third question arising from the other two: where is the writer when the reader is reading?

If you really are in the habit of reading other people's letters and diaries, you'll know the answer to that one straightaway: when you are reading, the writer is *not in the same room*. If he were, either you'd be talking together, or he'd catch you in the act.

For whom does the writer write? The question poses itself most simply in the case of the diary-writer or journal-keeper. Only very occasionally is the answer specifically *no one*, but this is a misdirection, because we couldn't hear it unless a writer had put it in a book and published it for us to read. Here for instance is diary-writer Doctor Glas, from Hjalmar Soderberg's astonishing 1905 Swedish novel of the same name:

> Now I sit at my open window, writing – for whom? Not
> for any friend or mistress. Scarcely for myself, even. I do
> not read today what I wrote yesterday; nor shall I read
> this tomorrow. I write simply so my hand can move, my
> thoughts move of their own accord. I write to kill a
> sleepless hour.[9]

A likely story, and it *is* a likely story – we, the readers, believe it easily enough. But the truth – the real truth, the truth behind the illusion – is that the writing is not by Doctor Glas, and it's not addressed to no one. It's by Hjalmar Söderberg, and it's addressed to us.

The fictional writer who writes to no one is rare. More usually, even fictional writers writing fictional journals wish to suppose a reader. Here is a passage from George Orwell's *Nineteen Eighty-Four*, a book I read as a young person, shortly after it first came out in 1949. As we know, *Nineteen Eighty-Four* takes place in a grimy totalitarian future ruled by Big Brother. The hero, Winston Smith, has seen in a junk-store window a forbidden object: 'a thick, quarto-sized blank book with a red back and a marbled cover' and 'smooth creamy paper.'[10] He has been seized by the desire to possess this book, despite the dangers that owning it would entail. Who among writers has not been overcome by a similar desire? And who has not been aware, too, of the dangers – specifically, the dangers of self-revelation? Because if you get hold of a blank book, especially one with creamy pages, you will be driven to write in it. And this is what Winston Smith does, with a real pen and real ink, because the lovely paper deserves these. But then a question arises:

> For whom, it suddenly occurred to him to wonder, was he writing this diary? For the future, for the unborn . . . For the first time the magnitude of what he had undertaken came home to him. How could you communicate with the future? It was of its nature impossible. Either the future would resemble the present, in which case it would not listen to him: or it would be different from it, and his predicament would be meaningless.[11]

A common writerly dilemma: who's going to read what you write, now or ever? Who do you want to read it? Winston Smith's first readership is himself – it gives him satisfaction to write his forbidden thoughts in his diary. When I was a teenager, this account of Winston Smith's blank book was intensely attractive to me. I too attempted to keep such a diary, without result. My failure was my failure to imagine a reader. I didn't want anybody else to read my diary – only I should have access to it. But I myself already knew the sorts of things I might put into it, and mawkish things they were, so why bother writing them down? It seemed a waste of time. But many have not found it so. Countless are the diaries and journals, most obscure, some famous, that have been faithfully kept through the centuries, or the centuries of pen and paper, at least. For whom was Samuel Pepys writing? Or Saint-Simon? Or Anne Frank? There is something magical about such real-life documents. The fact that they have survived, have reached our hands, seems like the delivery of an unexpected treasure; or else like a resurrection.

These days I do manage to keep a journal of sorts, more in self-defense than anything else, because I know who the reader will be: it will be myself, in about three weeks, because I can no longer remember what I might have been doing at any given time. The older one gets, the more relevant Beckett's play *Krapp's Last Tape* comes to be. In this play, Krapp is keeping a journal on tape, from year to year. His only reader – or auditor – is himself, as he plays back bits of the tapes from his earlier lives. As time goes on, he has a harder and harder time identifying the person he is now with his former selves. It's like that bad stockbrokers' joke about Alzheimer's Disease – at least you keep meeting new people – but in Krapp's case, and increasingly in mine, you yourself are those new people.

The private diary is about as minimalist as you can get, in the writer-to-reader department, because writer and reader are assumed to be the same. It is also about as intimate, as a form.

Next comes, I suppose, the private letter: one writer, one reader, and a shared intimacy. 'This is my letter to the World / That never wrote to me,' said Emily Dickinson.[12] Of course she might have got more replies if she'd mailed it. But she did intend a reader, or more than one, at least in the future: she saved her poems up very carefully, and even sewed them into little booklets. Her faith in the existence, indeed the attentiveness, of the future reader was the opposite of Winston Smith's despair.

Writers have of course made copious use of the letter as a form, inserting letters into the narrative, and in some cases building whole novels out of them, as Richardson did in *Pamela, Clarissa Harlowe*, and *Sir Charles Grandison*, and as Laclos did in *Les Liaisons dangereuses*. For the reader, the fictional exchange of letters among several individuals provides the delight of the secret agent listening in on a wire: letters have an immediacy that the past tense cannot provide, and the lies and manipulations of the characters can be caught *in flagrante delicto*. Or this is the idea.

A few words about letter-writing and the anxieties specific to it. When I was a child, there was a game that was popular at little girls' birthday parties. It went like this:

The children stood in a circle. One of them was It, and walked around the outside of the circle holding a handkerchief, while the others sang:

> I wrote a letter to my love
> And on the way I dropped it,
> A little doggie picked it up
> And put it in his pocket.

Then there was talk of dog-bites, and a moment when the handkerchief was dropped behind someone, followed by a chase around the outside of the circle. None of this part interested me. I was still worrying about the letter. How terrible that it had been lost, and that the person to whom it was written would never get it! How equally terrible that someone else had found it! My only consolation was that dogs can't read.

Ever since writing was invented, such accidents have been a distinct possibility. Once the words have been set down they form part of a material object, and as such must take their chances. The letter from the king that is exchanged, unknown to the messenger, causing an innocent person to be condemned to death – this is not merely an old folktale motif. Forged letters, letters gone astray and never received, letters that are destroyed, or that fall into the wrong hands – not only that, forged manuscripts, entire books that are lost and never read, books that are burned, books that fall into the hands of those who don't read them in the spirit in which they are written, or who do, but still resent them deeply – all these confusions and mistakes and acts of misapprehension and malice have taken place many times over, and continue to take place. In the lists of those targeted and imprisoned and killed by any dictatorship, there are always quite a few writers, whose works have reached – self-evidently – the wrong readers. A bullet in the neck is a very bad review.

But for every letter and every book, there is an intended reader, a true reader. How then to deliver the letter or book into the right hands? Winston Smith, writing his diary, finds he cannot be content with himself as his only reader. He chooses an ideal reader – a party official called O'Brien, in whom he believes he detects the signs of a subversiveness equal to his own. O'Brien, he feels, will understand him. He's right about this: his intended reader does understand him. O'Brien has already thought the thoughts that Winston Smith is thinking, but he's thought them in order to be prepared with the counter-moves, because O'Brien is a member of the secret police, and what he understands is that Winston is a traitor to the regime.

He proceeds to arrest poor Winston, and then to destroy both his diary and his mind.

O'Brien is a negative or demonic version of Writer-to-Dear Reader, that ideal one-to-one relationship in which the person reading is exactly the person who ought to be reading. A more recent variation of the Demon Reader has been created by Stephen King, who specializes in extreme paranoia – and since he has a different kind of paranoia for every taste, he has a special one just for writers. The book is *Misery*,[13] and in it a writer of suffering-heroine romances featuring a hapless maiden called Misery falls into the hands of a deranged nurse who styles herself 'your biggest fan.' Veterans of book-signings would know right then to run for the washroom and escape out the window, but our hero can't do that, because he's been incapacitated in a car crash. What his 'biggest fan' wants is to force him to write a book about Misery, just for her. Then, he realizes, she plans to bump him off so that this book will only ever have one reader – herself. It's a version of the sultan's-maze motif – used, among other places, in *The Phantom of the Opera*[14] – in which the patron of a work of art wishes to murder its maker so only he will possess its secrets. The hero of *Misery* escapes with his life after the required amount of guck has messed up the furniture, leaving us to reflect that the one-to-one Writer-to-Dear-Reader relationship can get altogether too close for comfort.

It is altogether too close for comfort as well when the reader confuses the writer with the text: such a reader wants to abolish the middle term, and to get hold of the text by getting hold of the writer, in the flesh. We assume too easily that a text exists to act as a communication between the writer and the reader. But doesn't it also act as a disguise, even a shield – a protection? The play *Cyrano de Bergerac*[15] features a large-nosed poet who expresses his love for the heroine by pretending to be someone else – but it is he who writes the eloquent letters that win her heart. Thus the book, as a form, expresses its own emotions and thoughts, while concealing from view the person who has concocted them. The difference between Cyrano and the book in general is that Cyrano gives vent to his own emotions, but the thoughts and emotions in a book are not necessarily those of the writer of it.

Despite the hazards a reader may pose, a reader must be postulated by a writer, and always is. Postulated, but rarely visualized in any exact, specific form – apart that is from the primary readers, who may be those named on the dedication page – 'Mr. W. H.,'[16] or 'my wife,' and so forth – or the group of friends and editors thanked in the acknowledgments. But beyond that, the reader is the great unknown. Here is Emily Dickinson on the subject:

> I'm Nobody! Who are you?
> Are you – Nobody – Too?
> Then there's a pair of us!
> Don't tell! – they'd advertise – you know!
>
> How dreary – to be – Somebody!
> How public – like a Frog –
> To tell one's name – the livelong June –
> To an admiring Bog![17]

'Nobody' is the writer, and the reader is also Nobody. In that sense, all books are anonymous, and so are all readers. Reading and writing – unlike, for instance, acting and theatregoing – are both activities that presuppose a certain amount of solitude, even a certain amount of secrecy. I expect Emily Dickinson is using 'Nobody' in both of its senses – in the sense of an insignificant person, a nobody, but also in the sense of the invisible and never-to-be-known writer, addressing the invisible and never-to-be-known reader.

If the writer is Nobody addressing the reader, who is another Nobody – that hypocrite reader who is his likeness and his brother, as Baudelaire remarked[18] – where do the dreary Somebody and the admiring Bog come into it?

Publication changes everything. 'They'd advertise,' warns Emily Dickinson, and how right she was. Once the catalog is out of the bag, the assumed readership cannot consist of just one person – a friend or a lover, or even a single unknown Nobody. With publication, the text replicates itself, and the reader is no longer an intimate, a one to your one. Instead the reader too multiplies, just like the copies of the book, and all those nobodies add up to the reading public. If the writer has a success, he becomes a Somebody, and the mass of readers becomes his admiring Bog. But turning from a nobody into a somebody is not without its traumas. The nobody-writer must throw off the cloak of invisibility and put on the cloak of visibility. As Marilyn Monroe is rumored to have said, 'If you're nobody you can't be somebody unless you're somebody else.'[19]

And then doubt sets in. The writer-while-writing and the Dear Reader assumed as the eventual recipient of this writing have a relationship that is quite different from that between the mass-produced edition and 'the reading public.' Dear Reader is singular – second-person singular. Dear Reader is a You. But once both book and Dear Reader become multiplied by thousands, the book becomes a publishing statistic, and Nobody can be quantified, and thus becomes a market, and turns into the great plural third-person Them, and Them is another thing altogether.

Becoming known to Them results in the condition known as Fame, and the attitudes to fame, and to being famous, changed radically from the end of the eighteenth century to the end of the nineteenth. In the eighteenth century, the readership was assumed to be educated, to have taste; Voltaire, for instance, saw his fame as a tribute to his talents, not as a minus factor. Even the early Romantics had nothing against fame; in fact, they longed for it. 'The Trumpet of Fame is as a tower of Strength the ambitious bloweth it and is safe,'[20] said John Keats in a letter. But by the end of the century, a bigger slice of the public was literate, the dreaded bourgeoisie – not to mention the even more dreaded masses – now determined how many copies would sell, publishing had become a business, 'fame' and 'popularity' were equated, and to have a small but discriminating readership now had a definite appeal.

This attitude persisted well into the twentieth century. Here is a Graham Greene character from *The End of the Affair* – a rather grubby novelist called Maurice Bendrix, who knows he is about to commit the art-for-art-influenced blunder of becoming a 'vulgar success.'[21] This is what he thinks as he prepares to be interviewed by a critic who wants to write him up for a literary journal:

> I knew too well . . . the buried significance he would discover of which I was unaware and the faults I was tired of facing. Patronizingly in the end he would place me – probably a little above Maugham because Maugham is popular and I have not yet committed that crime – not yet, but although I retain a little of the exclusiveness of unsuccess, the little reviews, like wise detectives, can scent it on its way.[22]

Greene is being satirical, but the attitude he is satirizing was real enough: popularity – too much of it – was still regarded as a crime if you aspired to being what used to be called a 'highbrow' writer. In Cyril Connolly's *Enemies of Promise*, too much failure and too much success are equally to be feared. Among the other things a young writer has to look out for are his own potential readers, because once you start comforting yourself with the idea that they at least love you no matter what the critics say, you're finished as a serious writer. 'Of all the enemies of literature, success is the most insidious,'[23] says Connolly. He then quotes Trollope: '"Success is a poison that should only be taken late in life, then only in small doses."'[24] It seems churlish to remark that only successful people ever say things like that; but Connolly expounds. He breaks success down into social success: not too bad, because it can provide material; professional success: the regard of one's fellow artists, on the whole a good thing; and popular success, a grave danger. This last he also divides into three: a writer may become popular for his entertainment value, for political reasons, or because he has the human touch. Of these, the political factor is the least fatal to art, he thinks, because politics are volatile and complacency is therefore unlikely. An entertainer does not benefit from informed criticism because nobody ever offers any; his fate is simply to 'go on and on until he wakes up one day to find himself obscure.'[25] But those with the human touch may be ruined as artists: Connolly says, 'Neither harsh reviews, the contempt of equals, nor the indifference of superiors can affect those who have once tapped the great heart of suffering humanity and found out what a goldmine it is.'[26]

Connolly was not alone in his analysis; in fact, by his time – and by mine – this attitude was endemic among those with ambitions as artists. Take, for instance, Isak Dinesen's story, 'The Young Man With the Carnation.' It begins with a writer called Charlie who has achieved a remarkable success with his first novel, which was about the struggles of the poor. Now he feels like a fraud, because he doesn't know what to write next; he's sick of the poor, he doesn't want to hear another word about them, but his admirers and the public have decided he's noble, and are expecting yet more and better things about the poor from his pen. If he writes about anything else, they will think he's superficial and hollow. No matter what he does, he feels, he will be doomed – doomed to disappoint – to disappoint the public, the great Them. He wouldn't even be able to commit suicide with impunity: 'Now he had had the glaring searchlight of renown set on him, a hundred eyes were watching him, and his failure or suicide would be the failure and the suicide of a world-famous author.'[27]

There is no writer who has achieved any success at all who has not confronted this package of doubts. Repeat yourself and satisfy Them, or do something different and disappoint Them. Or worse – repeat yourself to satisfy Them, and then be accused of repetition.

There are certain stories you read – usually quite early in life – that take on an emblematic quality for you. One of these for me is a Ray Bradbury story from *The Martian Chronicles*, the title of which is 'The Martian.' It goes as follows:

The Americans have colonized Mars, and part of it has been turned into a sort of retirement town. The original Martians are possibly extinct, or have taken to the hills. A middle-aged American couple, who have lost their young son Tom back on Earth, hear a knock on their door in the middle of the night. A small boy is standing in the yard. He looks like the dead son. The man sneaks down and unlocks the door, and in the morning there is Tom, all fresh and shining. The man guesses it must be a Martian, but the wife accepts Tom unquestioningly, and the man goes along with it because the facsimile is better than nothing.

All goes well until they travel into town. The boy doesn't want to go, and with good reason: shortly after they arrive he disappears, but another family suddenly recovers a daughter believed to be dead. The man guesses the truth – that the Martian is shaped by the desires of others, and by his own need to fulfill them – and goes to fetch Tom back. But the Martian can't change: the wishes of the new family are too strong for him. "'You are Tom, you *were* Tom, weren't you?'" the man asks plaintively. "'I'm not anyone, I'm just myself,'"[28] says the Martian. A curious statement; this equation of selfhood with nonentity.[29] "'Wherever I am, I am something . . .'" says the Martian. And so it proves. The Martian turns back into Tom, but the new family gives chase, and so do all the people the Martian passes as he runs away, with his mirror-like 'face like silver' shining in the lights of the town. Cornered, the Martian screams, face after face flitting across his own. 'He was melting wax shaping to their minds,' says Bradbury, 'his face dissolving to each demand.' He collapses and dies, a puddle of various features, unrecognizable.

Once I'd begun to publish books, and to see them reviewed – and to find that several people I didn't much recognize were running around out there with my name on them – this story took on a new significance. 'So that's it. My face is melting,' I thought. 'I'm really a Martian.' It does explain a lot. Keats praised negative capability,[30] and unless a writer has something of this quality, she will write characters that are mere mouthpieces for her own views. But if she has too much negative capability, doesn't she risk being turned into melting wax by the strength of her audience's desires and fears, interacting with her own? How many writers have put on other faces, or had other faces thrust upon them, and then been unable to get them off?

At the beginning of this chapter I raised three questions. The first was about writers and readers – for whom does the writer write?

The answers have included Nobody and the admiring Bog. The second question was about books. Considering the book's position as the intermediate point between writer and reader, what is the book's function, or its duty?

The use of the word 'duty' assumes something with a will of its own, and the book as autonomous creature is a literary notion worth examining. There's a department of the post office called the Dead Letter Office, for letters that can't be delivered. This term implies that all the other letters are alive; which is nonsense, of course, but nonetheless an ancient and pervasive way of thinking. For instance, the Bible has often been called the living Word of God. Another *for instance*: it was the fashion a few hundred years ago for male writers to speak of their pregnancy – got with wordchild by the Spirit, or even by the Muse, if you can wind your head around that kind of gender transposition: such writers would then describe the book's gestation and its eventual birth. Of course a book is nothing like a baby really – some of the reasons are scatological – but the convention of the living words has been persistent. Thus Elizabeth Barrett Browning, among many others: 'My letters! All dead paper . . . mute and white! – / And yet they seem alive and quivering . . .'[31]

One of my university professors, who was also a poet, used to say that there was only one real question to be asked about any work, and that was – is it alive, or is it dead? I happen to agree, but in what does this aliveness or deadness consist? The biological definition would be that living things grow and change, and can have offspring, whereas dead things are inert. In what way can a text grow and change and have offspring? Only through its interaction with a reader, no matter how far away that reader may be from the writer in time and in space. 'Poems don't belong to those who write them,' says the lowly poem-filching postman to the poet Pablo Neruda in the film *Il Postino*.[32] 'They belong to those who need them.' And so it is.

Everything used by human beings as a symbol has its negative or demonic version, and the most demonic version of the text with a life of its own that I can remember comes again from Kafka. There's a Jewish legend concerning the Golem, an artificial man who could be brought to life by having a scroll with the name of God inscribed on it placed in his mouth. But the Golem could get out of control and run amok, and then you were in trouble.[33] Kafka's story is a sort of Golem story. It's called 'In the Penal Colony,' and it revolves around a justice machine used by the administration to execute prisoners, who have not been informed beforehand of their crime. To start the machine up, a text with the sentence written on it – a sentence devised by the former commander of the colony, who is now dead – is inserted into the top. The sentence is a sentence in both senses of the word – it's a grammatical sentence, and it's the sentence imposed on the man to be executed. The justice machine then carries out its functions by writing the sentence with an array of pen-like glass needles, in intricate calligraphy and with many flourishes, on the actual body of the condemned man. The criminal is supposed to achieve illumination after six hours, when he comes to understand what is being written on him. '"Enlightenment dawns on the dullest,"' says the officer who worships this machine. '"It begins around the eyes. From there it spreads out . . . Nothing further happens, the man simply begins to decipher the script, he purses his lips as if he were listening."'[34] (This is a novel method of teaching reading, which has yet to be tested by the school system.)

The end of the story comes when the officer, realizing that the old letter of the law is now a dead letter, sacrifices himself to his own machine; but this time it doesn't work properly. Its cogs and wheels break off and roll away, but by now the thing has a life of its own and it just keeps on going, scribbling and jabbing, until the officer is dead.

In this story the writer is inhuman, the page is the reader's body, and the text is indecipherable. Poet Milton Acorn has a line that goes, 'as a poem erases and re-writes its poet,'[35] which also makes the text the active partner, but I doubt that Kafka's variation is quite what he meant.

More usually, the living word is presented in a much more positive light. In the theatre – particularly the Elizabethan theatre – there was often a moment at the end of a play at which the text stepped out of its frame, so to speak, and the play appeared for a moment to be no play at all, but alive in the same sense as its audience. One of the actors would advance out front and address the audience directly. 'Hello, I'm not really who you thought I was; actually I'm an actor, and this is a wig. Hope you enjoyed the play, imperfect though it was, and if you did, please treat us actors gently and give us some applause,' was what these speeches in effect were saying. Or there might be a prologue – again, apart from the main action – in which an actor said a few words about the play, and recommended it to the audience; and then stepped back into his frame again and became part of the *dramatis personae*.

These moments of recommendation, or of revelation and conclusion, were recreated by many writers of novels and longer poems in little vignettes, either as a prologue, or as an *envoi*, a sending off. The ancestry of the form is most obvious when a novelist is pretending that his book is some sort of play: Thackeray, for instance, has a section at the beginning of *Vanity Fair* called 'Before the Curtain,' in which he says his book is a puppet show within Vanity Fair itself – a fair that consists of the readers, among others – and he, the author, is only the Manager of the Performance. And at the end of the book he says, 'Come, children, let us shut up the box and the puppets, for our play is played out.' But in many prologues or *envois*, the writer reveals himself as the creator of the work, and writes what amounts to a defense of the book's character, like a letter accompanying a job application or something on a patent-medicine bottle, supposedly from a satisfied client.

Or, at the end of the story, the writer may send off his book as if waving goodbye to it as it sets out on a journey – he or she wishes it well, and sees it on its way; and he may say goodbye also to the reader who has been the silent partner and collaborator thus far on the journey. Prologue and *envoi* have a lot to say about the complex but intimate connection between writer and book, and then between book and reader. Quite frequently the book is little – 'Go, little book' – almost as if it is a child, who must now make its own way in the world; but its way – its duty – consists in carrying itself to the reader, and delivering itself as best it can. 'You understand,' says Primo Levi in a letter to his German translator, 'it is the only book I have written and now . . . I feel like a father whose son has reached the age of consent and leaves, and one can no longer look after him.'[36] One of the most disarming *envois* is by François Villon, the rascally and perennially broke fifteenth-century French poet, who instructed his poem to get a very urgent message through to a wealthy prince:

> Go my letter, make a dash
> Though you haven't feet or tongue
> Explain in your harangue
> I'm crushed by lack of cash.[37]

Other writers are less blunt; instead, they display a friendly concern for the reader. Here is the Russian poet Pushkin, saying a charming goodbye to the reader at the end of his poem, *Eugene Onegin*:

> Reader, I wish that, as we parted –
> whoever you may be, a friend,
> a foe – our mood should be warm-hearted.
> Goodbye, for now we make an end.
> Whatever in this rough confection
> you sought – tumultuous recollection,
> a rest from all its toils and aches,
> or just grammatical mistakes,
> a vivid brush, a witty rattle –
> God grant that from this little book
> for heart's delight, or fun, you took –
> for dreams, or journalistic battle,
> God grant you took at least a grain.
> On this we'll part; goodbye, again.[38]

Two of the earliest and also the most complete pieces of writing of this sort are by John Bunyan; they come at the front of Parts One and Two of *The Pilgrim's Progress*. The Part One prologue, 'The Author's Apology for his Book,' is more like an advertisement than anything else – these are the many good things this book can do for you, plus a list of the wholesome ingredients – but in the Part Two prologue, called 'The Author's Way of Sending Forth his Second Part of the "Pilgrim,"' the book has become a person:

> Go, now my little Book to every place,
> Where my first *Pilgrim* has but shown his Face,
> Call at their door if any say, 'Who's there?'
> Then answer thou, 'Christiana is here.'[39]

Bunyan then gives his book a list of detailed instructions; but the book becomes frightened of its assignment, and begins to answer back. Bunyan reassures it, and replies to its objections by telling it what to say in various difficult situations; and finally he tells it, or her, that no matter how wonderful she is, there will be some people that won't like her, because that's just the way it is:

> Some love no Cheese, some love no Fish, and some
> Love not their Friends, nor their own house or home;
> Some start at Pig, slight Chicken, love not Fowl,
> More than they love a Cuckoo or an Owl.
> Leave such, my Christiana, to their choice,
> And seek those who to find thee will rejoice . . .[40]

Useful and bracing advice for any book, I think. The Ancient Mariner has an auditor who cannot choose but hear, but not all narrators have such a glittering eye, or such luck. Bunyan concludes with a very Protestant, fiscally honest, frugal, cheap-for-the-price sort of prayer:

> Now may this little Book a blessing be,
> To those that love this little Book and me,
> And may its Buyer have no cause to say,
> His Money is but lost or thrown away . . .[41]

Christiana has turned back into a book, a book-as-object, and an object that is for sale.

Such transformations – from book to person, from person to book – are in fact quite common. They can also be quite double-edged. We all know that a book is not really a person. It isn't a human being. But if you are a lover of books as books – as objects, that is – and ignore the human element in them – that is, their voices – you will be committing an error of the soul, because you will be an idolator, or else a fetishist. This is the fate of Peter Kien, the protagonist of Elias Canetti's novel *Auto da Fé*.

Auto da fé means 'act of faith,' and refers to the mass burnings of 'heretics' once put on by the Inquisition. Kien is a collector of books, and loves their physical presence, though he detests novels – they have too much feeling in them. He loves these book-objects of his, but in a twisted way: he hoards them; and we know he's in spiritual trouble when he refuses to let a little boy who is hungry for knowledge read any of them, and instead kicks him downstairs.

Early in the book, Kien has a nightmare. The scene is a bonfire, combined with an Aztec-style human sacrifice, but when the victim's chest is cut open, instead of a heart, out comes a book – and then another book, and then another. These books fall into the flames. Kien tells the victim to close up his chest, to save the books, but no: more and more books pour out. Kien rushes into the fire to save them, but whenever he puts out his hand to save a book, he clutches a shrieking human being. "'Let me go,'" Kien shouts. "'I don't know you. What do you want with me! How can I rescue the books!'"[42]

But he's missed the point. The human beings in the dream *are* the books – they are the human element in the books. He hears the voice of God, which says, "'There are no books here,'" but he misinterprets it. At the end of the novel, all the books he has collected come to life and turn against him – they are his prisoners, he has locked them up in his private library, and now they want their messages set free; for, as I've said, books must travel from reader to reader in order to stay alive. Finally he sets fire to them, and himself along with them: an *auto da fé*, the fate of a heretic. As the books burn, he can hear their letters escaping from the Dead Letter Office he has created, out into the world again.

Sometimes the book is allowed to speak on its own behalf, without the writer's intervention. Here is a poem by Jay Macpherson, called simply 'Book.' Not only is this a talking book, it's a riddle, the answer to which is contained in its title.

> Dear Reader, not your fellow flesh and blood
> – I cannot love like you, nor you like me –
> But like yourself launched out upon the flood,
> Poor vessel to endure so fierce a sea.
>
> The water-beetle travelling dry and frail
> On the stream's face is not more slight than I;
> Nor more tremendous is the ancient whale
> Who scans the ocean floor with horny eye.
>
> Although by my creator's will I span
> The air, the fire, the water and the land,
> My volume is no burden to your hand.
>
> I flourish in your sight and for your sake.
> His servant, yet I grapple fast with man:
> Grasped and devoured, I bless him. Reader, take.[43]

As well as being a boat, a whale, and the angel who wrestled with Jacob and blessed him, the little book is the object of consumption in a communion meal – the food that may be devoured but never destroyed, the feast that renews itself as well as the feast-guests' link with the spiritual. The angel must not only be grappled with, it must be assimilated by the reader, so that it becomes a part of him or her.[44]

This brings me to my last question: where is the writer when the reader is reading? There are two answers to that. First, the writer is nowhere. In his small piece called 'Borges and I,' Jorge Luis Borges inserts a parenthetical aside about his own existence. '(If it is true that I am someone)' he says.[45] By the time we, the readers, come to read those lines, that's a very big *if*, because by the time the reader is reading, the writer may not even exist. The writer is thus the original invisible man: not there at all but also very solidly there, at one and the same time, because the second answer to the question – *Where is the writer when the reader is reading?* – is, 'Right here.' At least we have the impression that he or she is right here, in the same room with us – we can hear the voice. Or we can almost hear the voice. Or we can hear *a* voice. Or so it seems. As the Russian writer Abram Tertz says in his story 'The Icicle,' 'Look, I'm smiling at you, I'm smiling in you, I'm smiling through you. How can I be dead if I breathe in every quiver of your hand?'[46]

In Carol Shields's novel *Swann: A Mystery*,[47] about a murdered woman poet and also about her readers, we find out that the original versions of the dead woman's poems are no longer fully legible – they were written on scraps of old envelopes and got thrown into the garbage by mistake, which blurred them quite a bit. Not only that, a resentful connoisseur has gone around destroying the few remaining copies of the first edition. But several readers have luckily memorized the poems, or parts of them, and at the end of the book they create – or recreate – one of these poems before our very eyes, by reciting the fragments. 'Isis keeps Osiris alive by remembering him,' says Dudley Young.[48] 'Remembering' as a pun may of course have two senses – it is the act of memory, but it is also the opposite of dismembering. Or this is what the ear hears. Any reader creates by assembling the fragments of a read book – we can read, after all, only in fragments – and making them into an organic whole in her mind.

Perhaps you will remember the end of Ray Bradbury's futuristic nightmare, *Fahrenheit 451*.[49] All the books are being burnt, in favor of wraparound TV screens that allow for more complete social control. Our hero, who begins as a fireman helping to destroy the books,[50] becomes a convert to the secret resistance movement dedicated to preserving books and, along with them, human history and thought. At length he finds himself in a forest where the insurgents are hiding out. Each has *become* a book, by memorizing it. The fireman is introduced to Socrates, Jane Austen, Charles Dickens, and many more, all of them reciting the books they have assimilated, or 'devoured.' The reader has in effect eliminated the middle point of the triangle – the text in its paper version – and has actually become the book, or vice versa.

With this circuit complete, I will go back to the first question – for whom does the writer write? And I will give two answers. The first is a story about my first real reader.

When I was nine, I was enrolled in a secret society, complete with special handshakes, slogans, rituals, and mottoes. The name of this was the Brownies, and it was quite bizarre. The little girls in it pretended to be fairies, gnomes, and elves, and the grownup leading it was called Brown Owl. Sadly, she did not wear an owl costume, nor did the little girls wear fairy outfits. This was a disappointment to me, but not a fatal one.

I did not know the real name of Brown Owl, but I thought she was wise and fair, and as I needed someone like that in my life at the time, I adored this Brown Owl. Part of the program involved completing various tasks, for which you might collect badges to sew on to your uniform, and in aid of various badge-collecting projects – needlework stitches, seeds of autumn, and so forth – I made some little books, in the usual way: I folded the pages, and sewed them together with sock-darning wool. I then inserted text and illustrations. I gave these books to Brown Owl, and the fact that she liked them was certainly more important to me than the badges. This was my first real writer–reader relationship. The writer, me; the go-between, my books; the recipient, Brown Owl;

the result, pleasure for her, and gratification for me.

Many years later, I put Brown Owl into a book. There she is, still blowing her whistle and supervising the knot tests, in my novel *Cat's Eye*, for the same reason that a lot of things and people are put into books. That was in the 1980s, and I was sure the original Brown Owl must have been long dead by then.

Then a few years ago a friend said to me, 'Your Brown Owl is my aunt.' 'Is?' I said. 'She can't possibly be alive!' But she was, so off we went to visit her. She was well over ninety, but Brown Owl and I were very pleased to see each other. After we'd had tea, she said, 'I think you should have these,' and she took out the little books I had made fifty years before – which for some reason she'd kept – and gave them back to me. She died three days later.

That's my first answer: the writer writes for Brown Owl, or for whoever the equivalent of Brown Owl may be in his or her life at the time. A real person, then: singular, specific.

Here's my second answer. At the end of Isak Dinesen's 'The Young Man With the Carnation,' God's voice makes itself heard to the young writer Charlie, who has been so despairing about his work. '"Come," said the Lord. "I will make a covenant between Me and you. I, I will not measure you out any more distress than you need to write your books . . . But you are to write the books. For it is I who want them written. Not the public, not by any means the critics, but Me, Me!" "Can I be certain of that?" asked Charlie. "Not always," said the Lord.'[51]

So that is who the writer writes for: for the reader. For the reader who is not Them, but You. For the Dear Reader. For the ideal reader, who exists on a continuum somewhere between Brown Owl and God. And this ideal reader may prove to be anyone at all – any *one* at all – because the act of reading is just as singular – always – as the act of writing.

6

Descent:
Negotiating with the dead
Who makes the trip to the Underworld, and why?

O Great Ones, Princes of the Night,
Bright Ones, Gibil the furnace, Irra
war-lord of the Underworld . . .
stand by me in my divination.
By this lamb that I am offering,
may truth appear!
    Mesopotamian invocation[1]

Build then the ship of death, for you must take
the longest journey, to oblivion.
And die the death, the long and painful death
that lies between the old self and the new . . .

Oh build your ship of death, your little ark
and furnish it with food, with little cakes, and wine
for the dark flight down oblivion
    D. H. Lawrence, 'The Ship of Death'[2]

A winter hanging over the dark well,
My back turned to the sky,
To see if in that blackness something stirs,
Or glints, or winks an eye:

Or, from the bottom looking up, I see
Sky's white, my pupil head –

Lying with all that's lost, with all that shines –
My winter with the dead:

A well of truth, of images, of words.
Low where Orion lies
I watch the solstice pit become a stair.
The constellations rise.
         Jay Macpherson, 'The Well'[3]

What moves and lives
     occupying the same space
what touches what touched them
     owes them . . .

Standing knee-deep in the joined earth
of their weightless bones,
in the archeological sunlight . . .

standing waist-deep in the criss-cross
rivers of shadows,
in the village of nightfall,
the hunters silent and women
bending over dark fires,
I hear their broken consonants . . .
         Al Purdy, 'Remains of an Indian Village'[4]

Take for joy from the palms of my hands
fragments of honey and sunlight,
as the bees of Persephone commanded us.
         Osip Mandelstam, 'Take for joy from the palms of
         my hands'[5]

When I was a young person reading whatever I could get my hands on, I came across some old books of my father's, in a series called Everyman's Library. The endpapers of that date were a sort of William Morris design, with leaves and flowers and a lady in graceful medieval draperies carrying a scroll and a branch with three apples or other spherical fruit on it. Interwoven among the shrubbery there was a motto: 'Everyman I will go with thee and be thy guide, In thy most need to go by thy side.' This was very reassuring to me. The books were declaring that they were my pals; they promised to accompany me on my travels; and they would not only offer me some helpful hints, they'd be right there by my side whenever I really needed them. It's always nice to have someone you can depend on.

Imagine my consternation when some years later, and enrolled in a university course that required me to fill my gaps, Middle English among them – I discovered the source of this cuddly quotation. It was a medieval play called *Everyman*, in which Everyman is not on some pleasant country stroll but on his way to the grave. All Everyman's friends have deserted him, including Fellowship, who wanders off in search of a stiff drink as soon as he hears the proposed destination. The only loyal one is Good Deeds, who isn't up to the job of saving Everyman from the consequences of himself, being too feeble. However, Good Deeds has a sister called Knowledge, and it is Knowledge who offers to be the helpful guide on Everyman's ramble to the tomb, and who speaks the words I have just quoted.

The relationship between me and these books, then, was not as cosy as I'd once thought. In the light of their newly discovered context, the three round fruits toted by the Pre-Raphaelite lady looked positively sinister: I was acquainted by then with Robert Graves's book *The White Goddess*,[6] and I felt I could recognize the food of the dead.

I remain rather amazed at the long-ago editors of this series, and their choice of design and epigraph. What possible help did they think *Pride and Prejudice* and *Mopsa the Fairy* were going to be to me on my leisurely hike to the crematorium? – though when you come to think of it, I suppose we're all on the same train trip, and it's a one-way ticket, so you might as well have something good to read on the way. And some lunch too – that must be where the fruit comes in.

The title of this chapter is 'Negotiating with the dead,' and its hypothesis is that not just some, but *all* writing of the narrative kind, and perhaps all writing, is motivated, deep down, by a fear of and a fascination with mortality – by a desire to make the risky trip to the Underworld, and to bring something or someone back from the dead.

You may find the subject a little peculiar. It is a little peculiar. Writing itself is a little peculiar.

This hypothesis was suggested to me by several things. The first of them was a throwaway sentence in Dudley Young's book, *Origins of the Sacred*,[7] to the effect that the Minoan civilization which once flourished on Crete left remarkably few written texts, and this was possibly because the Minoans weren't overly afraid of mortality – writing itself being, above all, a reaction to the fear of death. Despite all the remarks about enduring fame and leaving a name behind them that are strewn about in the letters and poems of writers, I had not thought much about writing *per se* as being a reaction to the fear of death – but once you've got hold of an idea, the proofs of it tend to proliferate.

Here are a few of the citations drawn almost at random from the heaps of printed material piled on my study floor. 'They're all dead now,' begins Ann-Marie MacDonald's novel *Fall on Your Knees*.[8] 'That [her brothers] Thomas and Timothy were killed before she was born was another part of the reason Ruth Cole became a writer,' says John Irving in his most recent novel, *A Widow for One Year*.[9] And from Chekhov:

> When a man in a melancholy mood is left tête-à-tête with the sea, or any landscape which seems to him grandiose, there is always, for some reason, mixed with melancholy, a conviction that he will live and die in obscurity, and he reflectively snatches up a pencil and hastens to write his name on the first thing that comes handy.[10]

There are many other examples of this connection – not necessarily a fear of death, as in *Timor mortis conturbat me*,[11] but a definite concern with it – an intimation of transience, of evanescence, and thus of mortality, coupled with the urge to indite. But let us take the connection as given, or as given in enough instances to establish a working premise, and ask ourselves: why should it be writing, over and beyond any other art or medium, that should be linked so closely with anxiety about one's own personal, final extinction?

Surely that's partly because of the nature of writing – its apparent permanence, and the fact that it survives its own performance – unlike, for instance, a dance recital. If the act of writing charts the process of thought, it's a process that leaves a trail, like a series of fossilized footprints. Other art forms can last and last – painting, sculpture, music – but they do not survive as *voice*. And as I've said, writing is writing down, and what is written down is a score for voice, and what the voice most often does – even in the majority of short lyric poems – is tell, if not a story, at least a mini-story. Something unfurls, something reveals itself. The crooked is made straight, or, the age being what it is, possibly more crooked; at any rate there's a path. There's a beginning, there's an end, not necessarily in that order; but however you tell it, there's a plot. The voice moves through time, from one event to another, or from one perception to another, and things change, whether in the mind alone or in the outside world. Events take place, in relation to other events. That's what time is. It's one damn thing after another, and the important word in that sentence is *after*.

Narration – storytelling – is the relation of events unfolding through time. You can't hold a mirror up to Nature and have it be a story unless there's a metronome ticking somewhere. As Leon Edel has noted, if it's a novel, there's bound to be a clock in it.[12] He was the biographer of Henry James, one of the most time-conscious novelists that ever was, and so he ought to know. And once you've got clocks, you've got death and dead people, because time, as we know, runs on, and then it runs out, and dead people are situated outside of time, whereas living people are still immersed in it.

But dead people persist in the minds of the living. There have been very few human societies in which the dead are thought to vanish completely once they are dead. Sometimes there's a taboo against mentioning them openly, but this doesn't mean they're gone: the absence from conversation of a known quantity is a very strong presence, as the Victorians realized about sex. Most societies assign these dead souls to an abode, and sometimes to several abodes: if the soul after death is assumed to be divisible, or if there's more than one kind of soul, as among the ancient Egyptians, then each part or soul must have its own territory.

Societies also have a way of devising rules and procedures – 'superstitions,' they're now called – for ensuring that the dead stay in their place and the living in theirs, and that communication between the two spheres will take place only when we want it to.[13] Having the dead return when not expected can be a hair-raising experience, especially if they are feeling slighted and needy, or worse, angry. 'Remember me,' as the ghost of Hamlet's father commands,[14] is not the first such heavy injunction to be laid on the living by the dead, nor will it be the last. The unrequested arrival of a dead person is seldom good news, and may indeed be distinctly alarming. 'Tomorrow in the battle think on me,' says the ghost of murdered Clarence to Richard III. But to Richmond, Richard's adversary, the same ghost says, 'Good angels guard thy battle! Live, and flourish,'[15] for although the dead have negative powers; they have positive and protective ones as well. Consider Cinderella's dead mother, purveyor of ballgowns and glass slippers.

A lot of the superstitions, or rules and procedures, governing life death traffic involve food, because the dead are assumed to be hungry and unsatisfied. In Mexico, the Day of the Dead is, among other things, a feast day for dead people. In addition to the sugar skulls eaten by children, and the jolly tin assemblages depicting skeletons having a whale of a time doing all the things the living do – dressing up, playing music or cards, dancing and drinking – the family will prepare a special meal for its dead people, with all their favorite foods, and perhaps even a basin and towel so they can wash their invisible hands. In some communities the meal is eaten by the family itself, right on the grave; in others, a trail is made – of marigold petals, usually – from the grave to the house, so the dead person will be able to find his way to the meal, and also make his way back to his proper domicile after it. The dead are considered to be still part of the community, but they are not permanent residents. Even the most beloved one is only a guest, to be treated with honor, consideration, and a bite to eat, in return for which the dead person is expected to behave as a good guest should, and go home when the party's over.

These are not by any means extinct practices, and similar ones – or vestiges of them – are widespread. I was talking about these matters a while ago with someone from Greece. He described a custom whereby a certain kind of bread is baked – it's round in shape, as the food of the dead often is[16] – and on the day set aside for the dead, you are supposed to take this bread object to the ancestral tomb, and then persuade as many passing strangers as you can to take a nibble of it. The more strangers you corral, the better your luck will be in the coming year. Perhaps the strangers are the stand-ins for the dead, and giving them this special food is meant to propitiate them and ensure their support.[17] Similarly, in Japan and China and many other cultures the ancestors must be given their share, at least symbolically. If they feel they've been respected, they'll help you. If not – well, it's always best to be on the safe side.

Then there's our own Halloween, a remnant of the pre-Christian Celtic night of the dead – primarily, now, a North American phenomenon. The spirits are abroad, and you need protection, so you make a pumpkin with a goblin face and a light inside it, to act as the guardian of your threshold. The dead are represented by children wearing masks and costumes – it used to be ghosts, witches, and goblins, but today it's just as likely to be

Elvis Presley, Superman, or Mickey Mouse, whom we have apparently now claimed as ancestral spirits. These come to your door and demand food. 'Trick or treat' is one of the verbal formulae – which means that unless the spirits get the food, you'll get the mischief. Again, giving food to the dead is supposed to propitiate them and bring luck to the living, even if that luck consists only in the freedom from being annoyed.

We lived in an old house in rural Ontario during the 1970s, and this house was haunted – so the local people said, and so some visiting the house experienced while we were there – and we asked the lore-conscious woman from the farm across the road what to do. 'Leave food out overnight,' she said. 'Make them a meal. Then they'll know you accept them, and you won't be bothered.' We felt kind of silly, but we did it, and it worked. Or, as the German poet Rilke puts it in a slightly different way, in his *Sonnets to Orpheus*, 'Don't leave bread or milk on the table / At night: that attracts the dead.'[18]

It does make you thoughtful about Santa Claus and his milk and cookies on Christmas Eve, especially when you know that in Sicily the presents for the kiddies are brought on All Souls' Eve, not by a man in a red suit, but by the dead grandparents. Why should we be surprised? Santa Claus himself is from the Other Place, disguise it as we may by calling it the North Pole; and anyone from the Other Place – whatever we may name that other place – Heaven, Hell, Fairyland, the Underworld – will bring luck to us, or else keep us free from harm, only if given something in return – at the very least, our prayers and gratitude.

What else might the dead want? Various things, depending on the circumstances. Hamlet's father, for instance, wants revenge, nor is his desire unique: Abel's blood cried out from the ground after the first murder, thus giving us the first example of talking blood, though not the last.[19] Other body products that have been known to vocalize include bones and hair, as in folk-songs – consider the extremely widespread 'Twa Sisters of Binnorie'[20] – and folk-tales such as 'The Singing Bone,'[21] the bone in question being a murdered girl's leg-bone that becomes a flute.

Modern stories about forensic pathologists, such as Patricia Cornwell's thriller-heroine Kay Scarpetta, or forensic doctor–anthropologists such as the protagonist of Michael Ondaatje's latest novel, *Anil's Ghost*, are firmly of this tradition – such an old and persistent one because it's so elemental, inter-bound as it is with the desire for justice and the longing for revenge. When the blind old man in the Ondaatje novel 'reads' a skull with his fingers, it's a recap of a very ancient scene. The premise is that dead bodies can talk if you know how to listen to them, and they *want* to talk, and they want us to sit down beside them and hear their sad stories.[22] Like Hamlet laying a death-scene narrative injunction on his friend Horatio – 'in this harsh world draw thy breath in pain / To tell my story'[23] – they want to be recounted. They don't want to be voiceless; they don't want to be pushed aside, obliterated. They want us to know. The harp or other musical instrument made from the dead girl's hair in the 'Twa Sisters' ballad speaks for them all when it denounces the murderer by singing, 'Woe to my sister, false Ellyn.' As Shakespeare said – or rather, as Macbeth says – 'Blood will have blood.'[24]

But revenge and justice are not the only desires of the visitants from other worlds. Sometimes, as in many ballad apparitions – *my love she came all dressed in white*, and any other ex-inamoratas likely to materialize wistfully at your bedside before cock-crow – their desires are erotic, and they want you to go with them. Sometimes there's a demon-lover element.[25] Sometimes there's a contractual one – you've sold your soul, and the creditor has come to collect. If we could sum up what all of them want, in one word – a word that encompasses life, sacrifice, food, and death – that word would be 'blood.' And this is what the dead most often want, and it is why the food of the dead is often, though not always, round, and also red. Heart-shaped, more or less, and blood-colored, like Persephone's pomegranate.[26]

Here is Odysseus, making the necessary sacrifice to attract the spirits of the dead, in Book XI of the *Odyssey*:

> When I had finished my prayers and invocations to the
> communities of the dead, I took the sheep and cut their
> throats over the trench so that the dark blood poured in.
> And now the souls of the dead came swarming up . . .
> From this multitude of souls, as they fluttered to and fro
> by the trench, there came an eerie clamour. Panic drained
> the blood from my cheeks.[27]

As well it might. Odysseus sits beside the trench with drawn sword in hand, to keep any of the souls from drinking the blood until he gets what he wants, because he's there to do a negotiation, to make a trade. Of what he wants in return, more shortly.

The dead, then, are fond of blood. Animal blood will do, or for very special occasions, human blood. It's often the same thing gods want, not to mention vampires. So do think twice about Valentine's Day. I always do – I had a boyfriend once who sent me – in a plastic bag, so it wouldn't drip – a real cow's heart with a real arrow stuck through it. As you may divine, he knew I was interested in poetry.

One of the first request-by-the-dead poems I was ever exposed to was the most famous poem ever written by a Canadian: we all had to memorize it in school. It isn't usually thought of as a negotiate-with-the-dead poem – more as a pious commemoration verse; and so it duly made its appearance every year on

Remembrance Day, at the eleventh hour of the eleventh day of the eleventh month. The eleventh month is November, and my birthday is situated in it, which used to displease me because there wasn't anything you could put on the birthday cake, not like May with its flowers or February with its hearts; but then I found out that, astrologically speaking, November was the month governed by Scorpio, sign of death, sex, and regeneration. (This still wasn't much help with the birthday cakes.)

Why all three of these things together? What does death have to do with sex and regeneration? That's a whole footnote to itself; in fact, it may be a whole book to itself, the name of which might possibly be Frazer's *The Golden Bough*; but meanwhile, here's the poem – 'In Flanders Fields,' by John McCrae:

> In Flanders fields the poppies blow
> Between the crosses, row on row,
>   That mark our place; and in the sky
>   The larks, still bravely singing, fly
> Scarce heard amid the guns below.
>
> We are the Dead. Short days ago
> We lived, felt dawn, saw sunset glow,
>   Loved and were loved, and now we lie,
>   In Flanders fields.
>
> Take up our quarrel with the foe:
> To you from failing hands we throw
>   The torch; be yours to hold it high.
>   If ye break faith with us who die
> We shall not sleep, though poppies grow
> In Flanders fields.[28]

Note how the living are embedded in time, between dawns and sunsets, and how the Dead, capital D, are embedded out of time. Note the deal proposed by the Dead. Note the threat of retaliation if the terms are not respected: we'd better do as requested, because we wouldn't want any sleepless dead prowling around. You may think there's no food in this poem, apart from the poppies – round and red, like the food of the dead – but note what the Dead want. Yes, it's traditional: they want blood. They want the blood of the living, or at least they want that blood put at risk on behalf of their own cause.

At the time of its first publication, this poem was thought to be about the sustaining of belligerence toward enemy aliens during World War I. However, that is now over eighty years ago, and if this were all the poem ever said, it would long ago have run out of energy. But something powerful remains, because it embodies a very old and very strong pattern. The dead make demands, says the poem, and you can't just dismiss either the dead or the demands: you'd be wise to take both of them seriously.

Calling up the dead, and dealing with them across the threshold – because there always is a threshold, between our world and their world, and that's what those hex signs are doing on the old barns in Pennsylvania, and that's why you draw a circle around yourself if conjuring up the dead, and I suppose that's why Odysseus sat with drawn sword, because the spirits, in many traditions, can't pass metal – invoking these spirits, then, is one thing. At least you have some control over the situation. Even when the dead arrive uninvited, as in the Hamlet's-father and defunct-true-love scenarios, as a rule you know that if you can just last out until daybreak, they'll be gone. But there's something quite a lot riskier: instead of dealing with the dead on your own territory – merry middle-earth – you can cross over into theirs. You can go on a journey from this world to that. You can go down into the land of the dead, and then you can get out again,

back to the land of the living. But only if you're lucky. As the
Sibyl of Cumae tells Aeneas before they begin such a journey, in
Book VI of the *Aeneid*,

> . . . the way to Avernus is easy;
> Night and day lie open the gates of death's dark kingdom:
> But to retrace your steps, to find the way back to daylight –
> That is the task, the hard thing.[29]

In other words, this is a very tricky business – you might get
stuck down there – and it's also quite a test of your fortitude;
which is probably why so many heroes and heroines in the
Western tradition, and in many other traditions as well, have
undertaken it. Why do these heroes do it? Why take the chance?
Because the dead have some very precious and desirable things
under their control, down there in their perilous realm, and
among these are some things you yourself may want or need.

What sort of things? To summarize: (1) riches; (2) knowledge; (3) the chance to battle an evil monster; (4) the loved and
the lost. This list is not all-inclusive, but it includes the main
aims of such journeys. You can gain more than one thing at a
time, of course. You can get riches plus the loved and the lost,
or knowledge plus the fight with the monster, or any other
combination.

For 'riches,' I'll just mention fairy gold, that substance with
the unfortunate habit of turning to coal in the morning; and also
the riches controlled by the Chinese ancestors, for whom you
burn red paper money[30] in return for the real money you want
them to bring you. Then there are the sacrifices made so that the
dead will ensure a bountiful harvest: 'Give us this day our daily
bread,' that simple request in the Lord's Prayer, is a very modest
version of an invocation made to the Other World in the hope of
material welfare. Wealth of every kind flows from the invisible

world to the visible one, and the trance journeys made by the shamans of hunting societies in search of the locations of desired animals are based on this belief: the dead control the harvests, and they can tell you where the caribou are to be found.[31] The realm of the dead is a cavern of wonders, an Aladdin's treasure-trove. Like the abode of Eric, the very weird opera monster in *The Phantom of the Opera*, it's rich and strange; like the subterranean world of the not unrelated Grimms' fairy-tale, 'The Twelve Dancing Princesses,' down there the trees bear jewels for fruit. And like the treasure-chambers of Bluebeard, another Plutonic monster, the gold and jewels must be handled with great care, for death itself may have touched them.

The second thing I mentioned was knowledge. Because they are outside time, the dead know both the past and the future. 'Why have you called me up?' says the ghost of the prophet Samuel to King Saul, through the medium of the Witch of Endor.[32] King Saul has done this thing – a thing he himself has forbidden – because he wants to know what the coming battle has in store for him. (Nothing good, as it turns out.) Similarly, it's for knowledge of the future that Odysseus seeks out the ghost of the double-sexed seer Tiresias, and such knowledge is also the motive of Aeneas, who goes to the realm of the dead with the aid of the Sibyl of Cumae in order to learn all about the glorious future of his own descendants. (Macbeth wants the same thing, but it backfires; through the three Sibyls, now downgraded to nasty old witches, he learns all about the glorious future of somebody else's descendants.)

Knowledge and riches can be connected, of course – knowledge can be knowledge about how to get hold of the riches. One of the first modern short stories I ever read was D. H. Lawrence's classic, 'The Rocking-Horse Winner,' which has haunted me ever since. It's a complex story, but in relation to our subject it goes as follows. A beautiful woman has no luck with money, and does not really love her little boy. This little boy longs for some luck, so he can acquire the riches his mother desires; the implication is that by doing so he might also get some love from her. He has clairvoyant powers, and takes to riding his rocking-horse to put himself into a trance. When things go well, his horse takes him to 'where there is luck,' and he is able to learn the names of the winners in upcoming races. By this means he becomes rich, but he still doesn't get love. That the place 'where there is luck' is also the land of the dead becomes clear at the end of the story: the boy gets to the place, all right, but this time he isn't able to make the journey back, and he dies. Such a fate is always a possibility for journeyers to the Other World.[33]

The third item I mentioned was a battle with a monster. Among the shamans, the battle was usually a battle with a spirit, and if you won, the spirit would become your familiar, and if you lost, you'd become possessed by it. Or it could be a fight with the spirits of the dead for control of the harvest.[34] In myths that get into literature, things are usually narrowed down to one or two monsters per hero. There's Theseus and his labyrinth and Minotaur, of course, and Beowulf and his dark tarn and his Grendel's Mother. And there's Bilbo Baggins and his underground riddle-contest in Tolkien's *The Hobbit*, not to mention Gandalf and the Balrog in *Lord of the Rings*. And there's Christ, who during the three days between Good Friday and Easter Sunday goes down to Hell and defies the Devil, and rescues a group of good people who have been kept down there because until Christ's advent there hasn't been a redeemer to redeem them.

The fourth thing I mentioned was the quest for a lost beloved; this is an important motif when we're talking about writers and what drives them on. At first the vanished one may have been male: one of the most ancient seekers is the Egyptian goddess Isis, who sorrowfully gathers together the scattered body-parts of her slain husband Osiris, and by doing so restores him to life.

The Greek goddess Demeter pulls off a similar feat. She loses her daughter Persephone to Hades, the King of the Underworld; but she has a lot of bargaining power – she's the vegetation goddess, and she decrees that nothing will bear fruit again until the lost one is restored. Hades agrees to give Persephone back, on condition that she has eaten nothing while below ground. Unfortunately the girl has taken seven seeds from a pomegranate – one of those round, red foods of the dead. The prohibition against eating the food of the dead is enormously ancient –

> They will offer water from the river,
> Do not take the water of death.
> They will give you grain from the fields
> Of the dead, do not take that seed

says the Mesopotamian poem about the goddess Inanna's journey to Hell.[35]

In the Persephone story, as in the one about Inanna, her husband Dumuzi, and his sister Geshtinanna, a compromise is reached – part of the year in the Underworld, part above ground – and that's why we have winter.

Orpheus the musician and poet went in search of his dead wife Eurydice, and managed a successful negotiation with the rulers of the Underworld: he charmed them with his songs, and they agreed that he could have Eurydice back, just so long as he didn't look at her while leading her up to the land of the living. But he couldn't hold to his resolution, and so Eurydice went fluttering back to the dark halls. You should not eat the food of the dead, but also you should not question their take-home gifts too closely.

To go to the land of the dead, to bring back to the land of the living someone who has gone there – it's a very deep human desire, and thought also to be very deeply forbidden. But life of a sort can be bestowed by writing. Jorge Luis Borges, in his 'Nine Dantesque Essays,'[36] puts forward an interesting theory: that the entire *Divine Comedy*, all three sections of it – the *Inferno*, the *Purgatorio* and the *Paradiso* – this whole vast and intricate structure was composed by Dante mainly so he could get a glimpse of the dead Beatrice, and bring her back to life in his poem. It is because he is writing about her, and only because he is writing about her, that Beatrice is able to exist again, in the mind of writer and reader. As Borges says,

> We must keep one incontrovertible fact in mind, a single,
> humble fact: the scene was *imagined* by Dante. For us, it
> is very real; for him, it was less so. (The reality, for him,
> was that first life and then death had taken Beatrice from
> him.) Forever absent from Beatrice, alone and perhaps
> humiliated, he imagined the scene in order to imagine
> that he was with her.[37]

Borges then comments on the 'fleetingness of her glance and smile,' and 'the eternal turning away of the face.' How like the story of Orpheus this is – the poet, armed only with his poetry, enters the realm of the dead, traverses the Inferno, reaches the Elysian Fields or their equivalent, and finds the beloved again, only to lose her once more, this time for ever. As Dido turns away from Aeneas, as Eurydice turns away from Orpheus, thus Beatrice turns away from Dante. Never mind that it's toward God, never mind that she's happy – the essential thing *for him* is that she is lost. But regained again. But lost again. The end of the *Paradiso* is a happy ending only if we squint very hard.

And so it is with all happy endings of all books, when you come to think about it. You can't go home again, said Thomas Wolfe; but you can, sort of, when you write about it. But then you reach the last page. A book is another country. You enter it, but then you must leave: like the Underworld, you can't live there.

Virgil is usually assumed to be the first writer to have given us a full account of the Underworld in his function *as writer*. Note his short invocation in Book VI of the *Aeneid*:

> You gods who rule the kingdom of souls! You soundless
>   shades!
> Chaos, and Phlegethon! O mute wide leagues of
>   Nightland!
> Grant me to tell what I have heard! With your assent,
> May I reveal what lies deep in the gloom of the
>   Underworld![38]

Grant me to tell. May I reveal.[39] These are the prayers of a writer, and you'd almost think he'd been there himself. This is perhaps why Dante chooses the poet Virgil to be his guide in the *Inferno*: in visiting a strange location, it's always best to go with someone who's been there before, and – most important of all on a sightseeing tour of Hell – who might also know how to get you out again.

Rilke, in his *Sonnets to Orpheus*, makes the Underworld journey simply a precondition of being a poet. The journey must be undertaken, it is necessary. The poet – for whom Orpheus is the exemplary model – is the one who can bring the knowledge held by the Underworld back to the land of the living, and who can then give us, the readers, the benefit of this knowledge. 'Is he of this world? No, he gets / his large nature from both realms,' says

Rilke of the Orpheus poet in Sonnet 6 (Part I). In Sonnet 9 (Part I), he spells this out at more length:

> You have to have been among the shades,
> tuning your lyre there too,
> if you want vision enough to know
> how to make lasting praise.
>
> You have to sit down and eat
> with the dead, sharing their poppies,
> if you want enough memory to keep
> the one most delicate note . . .
>
> And the world has to be twofold
> before any voice can be
> eternal and mild.[40]

This poet doesn't just visit the Other World. He partakes of it. He is double-natured, and can thus both eat the food of the dead and return to tell the tale.

I said that Virgil is usually assumed to be the first *writer* to make the Underworld trip – that is, he makes the imaginary trip for the purpose of relating it. It, and all the other stories he gets told down there; and it's by the inmates of the *Inferno*, not in the *Purgatorio* or the *Paradiso*, that Dante is told the most stories, and also the best ones. It's somewhat daunting to reflect that Hell is – possibly – the place where you are stuck in your own personal narrative for ever, and Heaven is – possibly – the place where you can ditch it, and take up wisdom instead.

I would now like to propose a much earlier prototype for the subterranean adventurer as writer – the Mesopotamian hero Gilgamesh. Since the epic poem which contains him was not deciphered until the nineteenth century, he can hardly have been a direct influence on either Virgil or Dante; he is even more of a

test-case, then, for Dudley Young's thesis about the essential connection between the urge to write things down and the fear of
death.

In the first part of his story, Gilgamesh – a king who is half-
divine – is concerned mostly to make a name for himself, a name
that will outlast him. He has a companion, a tamed wild-man
called Enkidu, and together they accomplish heroic feats. But
they insult the goddess Ishtar – a sex-and-death goddess, as it
turns out – and thus Enkidu must die. He has to go down to the
extremely unpleasant Underworld of that time, where you ate
mud and were covered with frowsy bird-feathers.

Gilgamesh is deeply distressed: he can't get Enkidu back, and
in addition he is now afraid of death. So he sets out to find the
secret of eternal life, from the one mortal man who has never
died. The way leads over the wilderness and through the middle
of a dark mountain, and then through a garden where the trees
bear jewels for fruit, and then over the water of death. He finds
Utnapishtim, the immortal man, who tells him the story of the
flood and then gives Gilgamesh the key to eternal life; but
Gilgamesh loses it, and then he has to come all the way back to
his own kingdom again. Here is the end of his journey: 'He was
wise, he saw mysteries and knew secret things, he brought us a
tale of the days before the flood. He went on a long journey, was
weary, worn out with labour, and returning engraved on a stone
the whole story.'[41]

I was holding forth about this a while ago at a dinner for a bunch
of writers. 'Gilgamesh was the first writer,' I said. 'He wants the
secret of life and death, he goes through hell, he comes back, but
he hasn't got immortality, all he's got is two stories – the one
about his trip, and the other, extra one about the flood. So the
only thing he really brings back with him is a couple of stories.

Then he's really, really tired, and then he writes the whole thing down on a stone.'

'Yeah, that's what it is,' said the writers. 'You go, you get the story, you're whacked out, you come back and write it all down on a stone. Or it feels like a stone by the sixth draft,' they added.

'Go where?' I said.

'To where the story is,' they said.

Where is the story? The story is in the dark. That is why inspiration is thought of as coming in flashes. Going into a narrative – into the narrative process – is a dark road. You can't see your way ahead. Poets know this too; they too travel the dark roads. The well of inspiration is a hole that leads downwards.

'Reach me a gentian, give me a torch!' says D. H. Lawrence, that most chthonic of writers, in his poem, 'Bavarian Gentians.' 'Let me guide myself with the blue, forked torch of this flower / down the darker and darker stairs, where blue is darkened on blueness / even where Persephone goes . . .'[42] Yes, but why does the poet himself want to go down those dark stairs? It isn't a question he answers in the poem, but I'd guess it's not because he wants to die. Rather it's because he's a poet, and he must make such a descent in order to do what he does. He must partake of both realms, as Rilke claimed.

The Underworld guards the secrets. It's got the skeletons in the closet, and any other skeletons you might wish to get your hands on. It's got the stories, or quite a few of them. 'There is something down there and you want it told,'[43] as poet Gwendolyn MacEwen says. The swimmer among the jeweled dead – double-gendered, like the seer Tiresias – in Adrienne Rich's poem 'Diving Into the Wreck' has a similar motive:

> There is a ladder.
> The ladder is always there . . .

We know what it is for,
we who have used it . . .
I go down.

I came to explore the wreck.
The words are purposes.
The words are maps.
I came to see the damage that was done
and the treasures that prevail . . .

. . . the thing I came for:
the wreck and not the story of the wreck
the thing itself and not the myth[44]

The Québecoise poet Anne Hébert also wrote an astonishing poem along these lines. It's called 'The Tomb of Kings.' In it, a dreaming child – a girl, 'amazed, barely born' – goes down into a tomb, through an underground labyrinth, carrying her heart on her fist in the form of a blind falcon. Down there she finds the dead kings; she also finds their stories, 'a few patiently-wrought tragedies' which now appear as jeweled works of art. An exchange takes place – a vampiristic ritual in which the dead drink the living, and try to kill her. She shakes the dead away and frees herself; but as a result of whatever it is that has gone on, her heart – the blind bird – shows signs of being able to see.[45]

The dead get blood; as I said earlier, they are assumed to be hungry and thirsty. In return, the poet gets clairvoyance, and the completion of her identity as a poet. It's an old arrangement.

All writers learn from the dead. As long as you continue to write, you continue to explore the work of writers who have preceded you; you also feel judged and held to account by them. But you don't learn only from writers – you can learn from ancestors in all their forms. Because the dead control the past, they control the stories, and also certain kinds of truth – what Wilfred Owen, in his descent-to-the-Underworld poem, 'Strange Meeting,' calls the 'truth untold'[46] – so if you are going to indulge in narration, you'll have to deal, sooner or later, with those from previous layers of time. Even if that time is only yesterday, it isn't now. It isn't the *now* in which you are writing.

All writers must go from *now* to *once upon a time*; all must go from here to there; all must descend to where the stories are kept; all must take care not to be captured and held immobile by the past. And all must commit acts of larceny, or else of reclamation, depending how you look at it. The dead may guard the treasure, but it's useless treasure unless it can be brought back into the land of the living and allowed to enter time once more – which means to enter the realm of the audience, the realm of the readers, the realm of change.

We could go on to make explicit what has been implicit. We could talk about inspiration, or about trances and dream visions, or about charms and invocations – all of them linked with poetic traditions of long standing; then we could go one step further, and talk – as many have – about the shamanistic role of the writer. This may of course be a metaphor, but, if so, it does seem to be one that has held a central significance for writers over a very long period of time.

Such subjects can get murky or pretentious with astonishing rapidity, but I'll try to lend some respectability to the proceedings by leaving you with the words of a real scholar. This is from the Italian social historian Carlo Ginzburg's book, *Ecstasies: Deciphering the Witches' Sabbath*:

> Indubitable . . . is the deep resemblance that binds the myths that later merged in the witches' Sabbath. All of them work a common theme: going into the beyond,

returning from the beyond. This elementary narrative nucleus has accompanied humanity for thousands of years. The countless variations introduced by utterly different societies, based on hunting, on pasture and on agriculture, have not modified its basic structure. Why this permanence? The answer is possibly very simple. To narrate means to speak here and now with an authority that derives from having been (literally or metaphorically) there and then. In participation in the world of the living and of the dead, in the sphere of the visible and of the invisible, we have already recognized a distinctive trait of the human species. What we have tried to analyze here is not one narrative among many, but the matrix of all possible narratives.[47]

As the best authorities have it, easy to go there, but hard to come back; and then you must write it all down on a stone. Finally, if you are lucky and if the right reader comes along, the stone will speak. It alone will remain in the world to tell the story.

I will give the last word to the poet Ovid, who has the Sibyl of Cumae speak, not only for herself, but also – we suspect – for him, and for the hopes and fates of all writers:

But still, the fates will leave me my voice,
and by my voice I shall be known.[48]

Notes

Epigraphs

1. 'The Robber Bridegroom' is to be found in any standard edition of Grimms' Fairy Tales. The translation is mine. In this excerpt, the heroine is telling a true story in the guise of a dream.
2. Geoffrey Chaucer, 'The Millers Prologue,' from *The Canterbury Tales*, lines 3173–7, F. N. Robinson (ed.), *The Works of Geoffrey Chaucer* (London: Oxford University Press, 1957). The author is advising the reader who doesn't like what he's reading to read something else.
3. A. M. Klein, 'Portrait of the Poet as Landscape,' *The Rocking Chair and Other Poems* (Toronto: Ryerson Press, 1966), p. 55.

Introduction: Into the labyrinth

1. Elias Canetti, *The Agony of Flies* (New York: Farrar, Straus, and Giroux, 1994), p. 13.
2. Mavis Gallant, Preface, *Selected Stories* (Toronto: McClelland and Stewart, 1996), p. x.
3. Marguerite Duras, Mark Polizzotti (trans.), *Writing* (Cambridge, MA: Lumen Editions, 1993), p. 7.
4. Percy Bysshe Shelley, 'A Defense of Poetry' (1821), Donald H.

Reiman and Sharon B. Powers (eds.), *Shelley's Poetry and Prose: Authoritative Texts, Criticism* (New York: Norton, 1977).

5. James Reaney, 'The Bully,' Robert Weaver and Margaret Atwood (eds.), *The Oxford Book of Canadian Short Stories in English* (Toronto: Oxford University Press Canada, 1986), p. 153.

6. Ian McEwan, 'Reflections of a Kept Ape,' *In Between the Sheets* (London: Jonathan Cape, 1978), p. 438.

7. Reena is an acquaintance of the author.

8. Gallant, Preface, *Selected Stories*, p. ix.

1 Orientation: Who do you think you are?

1. E. K. Brown, 'The Problem of a Canadian Literature,' A. J. M. Smith (ed.), *Masks of Fiction: Canadian Critics on Canadian Prose* (Toronto: McClelland and Stewart, 1961), p. 47.

2. James Reaney, 'The Canadian Poet's Predicament,' A. J. M. Smith (ed.), *Masks of Poetry: Canadian Critics on Canadian Verse* (Toronto: McClelland and Stewart, 1962), p. 115.

3. Milton Wilson, 'Other Canadians and After,' *Masks of Poetry*, p. 38.

4. Alice Munro, 'Cortes Island,' *The Love of a Good Woman* (Toronto: Penguin, 1999), p. 143.

5. Kobo Abé, E. Dale Saunders (trans.), *The Woman in the Dunes* (New York: Vintage, 1964, 1972).

6. A. M. Klein, 'Portrait of the Poet as Landscape,' *The Rocking Chair and Other Poems* (Toronto: Ryerson Press, 1966), p. 50.

7. Northrop Frye said this frequently in lectures attended by the author during her undergraduate studies at the University of Toronto.

8. Elmore Leonard, *Get Shorty* (New York: Delta, Dell, 1990), p. 176.

9. Alice Munro, *Who Do You Think You Are?* (Agincourt, ONT.: Signet, 1978).

10. Ibid., p. 200.

2 Duplicity: The jekyll hand, the hyde hand, and the slippery double

1. Gwendolyn MacEwen, 'The Left Hand and Hiroshima,' *Breakfast for Barbarians* (Toronto: Ryerson Press, 1966), p. 26.
2. Nadine Gordimer, Introduction, *Selected Stories* (London: Bloomsbury, 2000), p. 4.
3. See Isaiah Berlin, Henry Hardy (ed.), *The Roots of Romanticism* (Princeton University Press, 1999).
4. *King Lear,* Act III, Scene iv.
5. Robert Browning, 'Childe Roland to the Dark Tower Came,' E. K. Brown and J. O. Bailey (eds.), *Victorian Poetry* (New York: Ronald Press, 1942, 1962), p. 220.
6. In Adelbert von Chiamisso's novel of the same name (London: Camden House, 1993). For a full account of romantic doubles, see Ralph Tymms, *Doubles in Literary Psychology* (Oxford: Bowes and Bowes, 1949).
7. Daryl Hine, 'The Doppelgänger,' *The Oxford Book of Canadian Verse* (Toronto: Oxford University Press, 1960), p. 318.
8. Charles Dickens, *The Old Curiosity Shop* (Ware, Hertfordshire: Wordsworth Editions, 1998).
9. E. L. Doctorow, *City of God* (New York: Random House, 2000), p. 65.
10. Isak Dinesen, 'A Consolatory Tale,' *Winter's Tales* (New York: Vintage, 1993), p. 296.
11. Patrick Tierney, *The Highest Altar* (New York: Viking, 1989).
12. The poet Dante Gabriel Rossetti uses this idea in his well-known picture, *How They Met Themselves.*
13. Oscar Wilde, *The Picture of Dorian Gray* (Ware, Hertfordshire: Wordsworth Editions, 1992).
14. William Fryer Harvey, *The Beast with Five Fingers* (New York: Dutton, 1947).
15. *Malleus Maleficarum* or *Hexenhammer* (1484), published by the Dominican inquisitor and the prior of Cologne, was the contemporary textbook on witchcraft.
16. Danny Shanahan, 'The moving finger writes, and having writ,

moves on to a three-week, twenty-city book tour,' *New Yorker*, February 21, 2000, p. 230.

17. Jorge Luis Borges, 'Borges and I,' James E. Irby (trans.), *Everything and Nothing* (New York: New Directions, 1999), pp. 74–5.

18. Robertson Davies, *The Merry Heart: Robertson Davies Selections 1980–1995*, (Toronto: McClelland and Stewart, 1996), p. 358.

19. See Leigh Hunt's poem, 'About Ben Adhem,' anthologized in *The Book of Gems* (1838), David Jesson-Dibley (ed.), *Selected Writings* (Manchester: Fyfield Books, 1990); see also the many war memorials in which an angel holds a book, in which, we may assume, the names of the blessed are written.

20. Except for St. John's gospel 8: 6–8, where he writes on the ground with his finger. But we aren't told what he writes.

21. Edgar Allan Poe, 'The Purloined Letter,' *Selected Writings of Edgar Allan Poe* (Boston: Houghton Mifflin Company, 1956).

22. Revelation 22: 18–19.

23. Walter Benjamin, 'The Work of Art in the Age of Mechanical Reproduction,' Hannah Arendt (ed.), *Illuminations* (New York: Schocken Books, 1969).

24. See Berlin, *The Roots of Romanticism*.

25. In the legends of ouiskijek, the trickster, who punished his own asshole for speaking out of turn.

26. William S. Burroughs, *The Naked Lunch* (New York: Grove Press, 1992).

27. Wilde, *The Picture of Dorian Gray*, p. 47.

28. Dinesen, 'A Consolatory Tale,' p. 309.

29. Primo Levi, *The Periodic Table* (New York: Schocken Books, 1984), pp. 232–3.

3 Dedication: The Great God Pen

1. Théophile Gautier, Preface, *Mademoiselle de Maupin* (New York: Modern Library, 1920), p. xxv.

2. Anna Akhmatova, 'The Muse,' Stanley Kunitz with Max

Hayward (trans.), *Poems of Akhmatova* (Boston: Atlantic Monthly Press, 1973), p. 79.

3. Rainer Maria Rilke, '26, [But you, godlike, beautiful],' David Young (trans.), *Sonnets to Orpheus*, Part I (Hanover, NH: Wesleyan University Press, 1987), p. 53.

4. Irving Layton, Foreword, *A Red Carpet for the Sun* (Toronto: McClelland and Stewart, 1959).

5. Henry James, *The Lesson of the Master and Other Stories* (London: John Lehmann, 1948), p. 60.

6. Elmore Leonard, *Get Shorty* (New York: Delta, Dell, 1990), p. 313.

7. Maxwell Perkins (1884–1947), as editor-in-chief of Scribners, was the archetypal nurturing editor who published works by Ernest Hemingway, F. Scott Fitzgerald, and Thomas Wolfe. The character of Foxhall Edwards in Wolfe's *You Can't Go Home Again* (1941) is thought to be based on him.

8. A paraphrase of the well-known couplet, 'He who fights and runs away / Will live to fight another day.'

9. Cyril Connolly, *Enemies of Promise* (Harmondsworth, Middlesex: Penguin, 1961).

10. James Joyce, *A Portrait of the Artist as a Young Man* (New York: Penguin, 1993), p. 241.

11. Eudora Welty, 'The Petrified Man,' *Selected Stories of Eudora Welty* (New York: The Modern Library, 1943), p. 55.

12. Lewis Hyde, *The Gift: Imagination and the Erotic Life of Property* (New York: Vintage, Random House, 1979, 1983).

13. Isak Dinesen, 'Tempests,' *Anecdotes of Destiny* (London: Penguin, 1958), p. 72.

14. 'Lord, I am not worthy,' Matthew 8: 8.

15. John 8: 32.

16. See John Keats, 'Ode on a Grecian Urn,' Douglas Bush (ed.), *Selected Poems and Letters* (Cambridge, MA: Riverside Press, 1959).

17. For a definitive and condensed treatment of this conflict, see Henry James's story, 'The Author of *Beltraffio*,' first published in 1884. See also chapter 4.

18. Alfred, Lord Tennyson, 'The Palace of Art,' George Benjamin

Woods and Jerome Hamilton (eds.), *Poetry of the Victorian Period* (Chicago: Scott, Foresman, 1930, 1955).

19. Ibid.
20. Oscar Wilde, *The Picture of Dorian Gray* (Ware, Hertfordshire: Wordsworth Editions, 1992).
21. Jorge Luis Borges, Esther Allen (trans.), 'Flaubert and his Exemplary Destiny,' Eliot Weinberger (ed.), *The Total Library: Non-Fiction 1922–1986* (London: Allen Lane, Penguin Press, 1999) p. 392.
22. The banner with the strange device is in Longfellow's poem 'Excelsior,' so devastatingly illustrated by cartoonist James Thurber.
23. Wilde, Preface, *Dorian Gray*, pp. 3–4.
24. Ralph Waldo Emerson, 'The Rhodora,' Reginald L. Cook (ed.), *Ralph Waldo Emerson: Selected Prose and Poetry* (New York: Rinehart, 1950), p. 370.
25. Wilde, Preface, *Dorian Gray*, p. 3.
26. Joyce, *Portrait of the Artist*, p. 215.
27. Elizabeth Barrett Browning, 'A Musical Instrument,' E. K. Brown and J. O. Bailey (eds.), *Victorian Poetry, Second Edition* (New York: Ronald Press 1962).
28. D. H. Lawrence, 'Song of a Man Who Has Come Through,' *Look We Have Come Through!* (New York: B. W. Huebsc, 1920).
29. Rilke, '3 [A god can do it. But tell me how],' *Sonnets to Orpheus*, Part I, p. 7.
30. Wilde, Preface, *Dorian Gray*, p. 3.
31. William Wordsworth, 'Resolution and Independence,' stanza 7, Stephen Gill and Duncan Wu (eds.), *William Wordsworth: Selected Poetry* (Oxford University Press, 1998).
32. Franz Kafka, 'A Fasting-Artist,' Malcolm Pasley (trans.), *The Transformation and Other Stories* (London: Penguin 1992), p. 219.
33. George Gissing, E. J. Taylor (ed.), *New Grub Street* (London: Everyman, 1997), p. 7.
34. Ibid., p. 452.
35. Ibid., p. 459.

36. Dinesen, 'Tempests,' *Anecdotes*, pp. 145–6.
37. 'Sibyl,' as in the prophetess beloved by Apollo, who doesn't come across and ends up in a bottle; 'Vane' as in weathervane, and vanity, and 'in vain.'
38. Robert Graves, *The White Goddess: A Historical Grammar of Poetic Myth* (London: Faber and Faber, 1952), p. 431.
39. In Samuel Taylor Coleridge, 'The Rime of the Ancient Mariner,' *The Rime of the Ancient Mariner and Other Poems* (New York: Dover, 1992), cited by Robert Graves.
40. George Eliot, *Daniel Deronda* (Oxford University Press, 1988), p. 536.
41. Ibid., p. 537.
42. Ibid., p. 543.
43. Layton, Foreword, *A Red Carpet for the Sun*.
44. Germaine Greer, *Slip-Shod Sibyls: Recognition, Rejection and the Woman Poet* (London: Penguin, 1995).
45. Sylvia Plath, 'Kindness,' February 1963, *The Collected Poems* (New York: Harper and Row, 1981), pp. 269–70.
46. The reference is to John Bunyan, Roger Sharrock (ed.), *The Pilgrim's Progress* (London: Penguin, 1965, 1987).

4 Temptation: Prospero, the Wizard of Oz, Mephisto & Co.

1. Voltaire, quoted in Nancy Mitford's *Voltaire in Love* (London: Hamish Hamilton, 1957), p. 174.
2. Ibid., p. 160.
3. Maurice Hewlett, *The Forest Lovers* (London: Macmillan 1899), p. 2.
4. Edith Sitwell quoted in Victoria Glendinning's *Edith Sitwell* (London: Phoenix, 1981), p. 140.
5. Cyril Connolly, *Enemies of Promise* (London: Penguin, 1961), p. 109.
6. A. M. Klein, 'Portrait of the Poet as Landscape,' *The Rocking Chair and Other Poems* (Toronto: Ryerson Press, 1966), p. 53.
7. Gwendolyn MacEwen, *Julian the Magician* (Toronto: Macmillan, 1963), p. 6.

8. Henry James, 'The Author of *Beltraffio,' In the Cage and Other Tales* (London: Rupert Hart-Davis, 1958), p. 56.

9. George Eliot, *Daniel Deronda* (Oxford University Press, 1988), p. 224.

10. Baron Edward Bulwer-Lytton, *Richelieu*, Act I, Scene ii (London: Saunders and Otley, 1839), p. 39.

11. Percy Bysshe Shelly, 'A Defense of Poetry,' Donald H. Reiman and Sharon B. Powers (eds.), *Shelley's Poetry and Prose: Authoritative Texts, Criticism* (New York: Norton, 1977), p. 508.

12. James Joyce, *A Portrait of the Artist as a Young Man* (New York: Penguin, 1993), p. 247.

13. Don De Lillo *Mao II* (New York: Penguin, 1991), p. 101.

14. Mavis Gallant, 'A Painful Affair,' *The Selected Short Stories of Mavis Gallant* (Toronto: McClelland and Stewart, 1996), p. 835.

15. Klein, 'Portrait of the Poet as Landscape,' *The Rocking Chair*, p. 50.

16. Susan Sontag in an interview with Joan Acocella, 'The Unquiet American,' *Observer*, 5 March, 2000.

17. Alice Munro, 'Material,' *Something I've Been Meaning to Tell You* (Toronto: McGraw Hill Ryerson, 1974), p. 35.

18. Ibid., p. 43.

19. Ibid., p. 44.

20. De Lillo, *Mao II*, p. 158.

21. Archibald MacLeish, 'Ars Poetica', *Collected Poems 1917–1982* (Boston: Houghton Mifflin, 1985), pp. 106–7.

22. Gertrude Stein, *Four Saints in Three Acts, Gertrude Stein: Writings 1903–1932* (New York: Library of America, 1998), p. 637.

23. Valerie Martin.

24. See Rosemary Sullivan's introduction to Gwendolyn MacEwen, Margaret Atwood and Barry Callaghan (eds.), *The Poetry of Gwendolyn MacEwen: The Later Years* (Toronto: Exile Editions, 1994).

25. L. Frank Baum, *The Wizard of Oz* (London: Puffin, 1982), p. 140.

26. Klaus Mann, *Mephisto* (Hamburg: Rowohlt, 1982), p. 77. My translation.

27. George Orwell, 'Why I Write,' *The Penguin Essays of George Orwell* (London: Penguin, 1968), p. 13.

28. Job 1: 15–19.

29. Henry James, *The Sacred Fount* (New York: New Directions, 1995), p. ix.

30. Kenneth McRobbie, *Eyes Without A Face* (Toronto: Gallery Editions, 1960).

31. Brian Moore, *An Answer From Limbo* (Boston: Atlantic, Little, Brown, 1992), p. 322.

32. Adrienne Rich, 'From the Prison House,' *Diving into the Wreck* (New York: Norton, 1973), p. 17.

5 Communion: Nobody to Nobody

1. Henry Fielding, *Tom Jones* (New York: Signet, Penguin, 1963, 1979), pp. 24–5.

2. Walter Benjamin, 'The Storyteller,' Hannah Arendt (ed.), *Illuminations* (New York: Schocken Books, 1969), p. 100.

3. Peter Gay, *The Pleasure Wars* (New York: Norton, 1998), p. 39.

4. Gwendolyn MacEwen, 'The Choice,' *The Rising Fire* (Toronto: Contact Editions, 1963), p. 71.

5. Henry James, 'The Death of the Lion,' *The Lesson of the Master and Other Stories* (London: John Lehmann, 1948). p. 86.

6. Anne Michaels, 'Letters from Martha,' *Miner's Pond, The Weight of Oranges, Skin Divers* (London: Bloomsbury, 2000), pp. 32–3.

7. John Le Carré, *Smiley's People* (New York: Bantam, 1974).

8. What he actually said was, 'The poet is not heard, he is over-heard.' Northrop Frye said this frequently in lectures attended by the author during her undergraduate studies at the University of Toronto.

9. Hjalmar Söderberg, Paul Britten Austin (trans.), *Doctor Glas* (first published 1905) (London: Tandem, 1963), p. 16.

10 George Orwell, *Nineteen Eighty-Four* (Harmondsworth, Middlesex: Penguin, 1949), pp. 8–9.

11. Ibid., p. 10.

12. Emily Dickinson, '441 [This is my letter to the World],' Thomas H. Johnson (ed.), *The Complete Poems of Emily Dickinson* (Boston: Little, Brown, 1890, 1960), p. 211.

13. Stephen King, *Misery* (New York: Viking, Penguin, 1987).

14. Gaston Leroux, *The Phantom of the Opera* (New York: HarperCollins, 1988).

15. Edmond Rostand, *Cyrano de Bergerac* (first published 1897) (New York: Bantam, 1954).

16. Dedicatee of *Shakespeare's Sonnets.*

17. Dickinson, '288 [I'm Nobody! Who are you?],' *Complete Poems*, p. 133.

18. 'Hypocrite reader! – You! – My twin! – My brother!' Charles Baudelaire, 'To the Reader,' Roy Campbell (trans.), *Flowers of Evil* (Norfolk, USA: New Directions, 1955), p. 4.

19. Marilyn Monroe, as mentioned in various biographical pieces.

20. John Keats, Letter to Benjamin Robert Haydon, May 10–11, 1817, Douglas Bush (ed.), *Selected Poems and Letters* (Cambridge, MA: Riverside Press, 1959).

21. Graham Greene, *The End of the Affair* (New York: Penguin, 1999), p. 129.

22. Ibid., p. 148.

23. Cyril Connolly, *Enemies of Promise* (Harmondsworth, Middlesex: Penguin, 1961), p. 129.

24. Ibid., p. 134.

25. Ibid., p. 133.

26. Ibid.

27. Isak Dinesen, 'The Young Man With the Carnation,' *Winter's Tales* (New York: Vintage, 1993), p. 4.

28. Ray Bradbury, 'The Martian,' *The Martian Chronicles* (New York: Bantam, 1946, 1977) p. 127.

29. It is worth noting in relation to chapter 2 that Borges was a fan of *The Martian Chronicles*. See Jorge Luis Borges, 'Ray Bradbury: The Martian Chronicles,' Eliot Weinberger (ed., trans.), *The Total Library: Non-Fiction 1922–1986* (London: Allen Lane, Penguin Press, 1999), pp. 418–19.

30. Keats defined negative capability as: '. . . when man is capable

of being in uncertainties, mysteries, doubts, without any irritable reaching after fact and reason.' Letter to George and Thomas Keats, December 22, 1817, *Selected Poems and Letters.*

31.   Elizabeth Barrett Browning, 'Sonnets from the Portuguese,' xxviii, E. K. Brown and J. O. Bailey (eds.), *Victorian Poetry* (New York: Ronald Press, 1962).

32.   *Il Postino,* Written by Massimo Troisi et al., directed by Michael Radford.

33.   Eduard Petiska and Jana Svábová (trans.), *Golem* (Prague: Martin, 1991).

34.   Franz Kafka, 'In the Penal Colony,' *The Transformation and Other Stories* (London: Penguin, 1992), p. 137.

35.   Milton Acorn, 'Knowing I Live in a Dark Age,' Margaret Atwood (ed.), *The New Oxford Book of Canadian Verse in English* (Toronto: Oxford University Press Canada, 1982), p. 238.

36.   Primo Levi, Raymond Rosenthal (trans.), *The Drowned and the Saved* (London: Abacus, 1999), p. 142.

37.   François Villon, 'Ballade [My lord and fearsome prince],' Galway Kinnell (ed.), *The Poems of François Villon* (Boston: Houghton Mifflin, 1977), p. 197.

38.   Alexander Pushkin, 'Eugene Onegin,' Avraham Yarmolinsky (ed.), *The Poems, Prose and Plays of Alexander Pushkin* (New York: The Modern Library, 1936), p. 301.

39.   John Bunyan, Roger Sharrock (ed.), *The Pilgrim's Progress* (London: Penguin, 1987), p. 147.

40   Ibid., pp. 151–2.

41.   Ibid., p. 153.

42.   Elias Canetti, *Auto da Fé* (New York: Picador, Pan Books, 1978), p. 35.

43.   Jay Macpherson, 'Book,' Robert Weaver and William Toye (eds.), *The Oxford Anthology of Canadian Literature* (Toronto: Oxford University Press Canada, 1973), p. 322.

44.   The word as food is an ancient concept. Christ in the New Testament is the Word made Flesh, and the flesh is the flesh of the Communion meal. See also the edible scroll (Isaiah 34: 4) and the edible book (Revelation 10: 8–10). And for sheer

pleasure, see the Prologue to *Tom Jones*, in which Fielding presents a Bill of Fare for his book, which he likens to a meal at an inn. Henry Fielding, *Tom Jones* (New York: Signet, Penguin, 1963, 1979).

45. Jorge Luis Borges, 'Borges and I,' James E. Irby (trans.), *Everything and Nothing* (New York: New Directions, 1999), p. 74.

46. Abram Tertz, 'The Icicle,' *The Icicle and Other Stories* (London: Collins and Harvill, 1963).

47. Carol Shields, *Swann: A Mystery* (Toronto: Stoddart, 1987).

48. Dudley Young, *Origins of the Sacred: The Ecstasies of Love and War* (New York: St. Martin's Press, 1991), p. 325.

49. Ray Bradbury, *Fahrenheit 451* (New York: Ballantine Books, 1995).

50. Compare the memory-hole in Orwell, *Nineteen Eighty-Four*, and the book destruction in Bohumile Hrabal, Michael Henry Heim (trans.), *Too Loud a Solitude* (London: Abacus, 1990) or in Ursula K. LeGuin, *The Telling* (New York: Harcourt, 2000).

51. Dinesen, 'The Young Man With the Carnation,' p. 25. Many writers have of course felt they wrote by order of God, or some god – the one that has most recently come to my attention is Canadian novelist Margaret Laurence, who confessed this to fellow writer Matt Cohen. See *Typing* (Toronto: Knopf Canada, 2000), p. 186.

6 Descent: Negotiating with the dead

1. N. K. Sandars (trans.), 'A Prayer to the Gods at Night,' *Poems of Heaven and Hell from Ancient Mesopotamia* (London: Penguin, 1971), p. 175.

2. D. H. Lawrence, 'The Ship of Death,' Richard Ellmann and Robert O'Clair (eds.), *The Norton Anthology of Modern Poetry*, second edition (New York: Norton, 1988), pp. 372–3.

3. Jay Macpherson, 'The Well,' *Poems Twice Told: The Boatman and Welcoming Disaster* (Toronto: Oxford University Press, 1981), p. 83.

4. Al Purdy, 'Remains of an Indian Village,' *Beyond Remembering: The Collected Poems of Al Purdy* (Madeira Park, BC: Harbour Publishing, 2000), p. 53.

5. Osip Mandelstam, '[Take for joy from the palms of my hands],' *Selected Poems* (New York: Farrar, Straus, and Giroux, 1975), p. 67.

6. Robert Graves, *The White Goddess: A Historical Grammar of Poetic Myth* (London: Faber and Faber, 1952).

7. Dudley Young, *Origins of the Sacred: The Ecstasies of Love and War* (New York: St. Martin's Press, 1991).

8. Ann-Marie MacDonald, *Fall on Your Knees* (Toronto: Alfred A. Knopf, 1996), p. 1.

9. John Irving, *A Widow for One Year* (Toronto: Alfred A. Knopf, 1998), p. 6.

10. Anton Chekhov, Ronald Hingley (ed. and trans.), 'Lights,' *The Oxford Chekhov Volume IV: Stories 1888–1889* (Oxford University Press, 1980), p. 208.

11. 'The fear of death unsettles me,' from 'Lament for the Makaris' by William Dunbar (c. 1465–1513).

12. Edel in conversation with Graeme Gibson.

13. For more on this subject, see Claude Lévi-Strauss and Wendy Doniger, *Myth and Meaning* (New York: Schocken Books, 1995).

14. Spoken by the ghost of Hamlet's murdered father, William Shakespeare, *Hamlet*, Act I, Scene v.

15. William Shakespeare, *Richard III*, Act V, Scene iii.

16. Consider the oranges offered in China to the dead.

17. See W. G. Sebald, Michael Hulse (trans.), *Vertigo* (New York: New Directions, 2000), pp. 64–5.

18. Rainer Maria Rilke, '6 [Is he of this world? No, he gets],' David Young (trans.), *Sonnets to Orpheus*, Part I (Hanover, NH: Wesleyan University Press, 1987), p. 13.

19. See for instance the three drops of talking blood in the Brothers Grimm, 'The Goose Girl,' Padraic Colum (intro.), *The Complete Grimms' Fairy Tales* (New York: Pantheon, 1972), pp. 404–11.

20. Francis James Child (ed.), 'The Twa Sisters,' *The English and*

Scottish Popular Ballads (New York: Dover, no copyright date given), vol. I, p. 128.

21. Brothers Grimm, 'The Singing Bone,' Padraic Colum (intro.), *The Complete Grimms' Fairy Tales*, pp. 148–50.

22. See the anonymous folk-song, 'The Streets of Laredo.'

23. *Hamlet*, Act V, Scene ii.

24. *Macbeth*, Act II, Scene iv.

25. See, for instance, Elizabeth Bowen, 'The Demon Lover,' *The Demon Lover and Other Stories* (London: Jonathan Cape, 1945).

26. See Louise Glück, 'Pomegranate,' *The House on Marshland* (Hopewell, NJ: Ecco Press, 1971, 1975), p. 28. See also the red blood–wine and the round wafer–body of the Christian Communion Sacrament.

27. Homer, E. V. Rieu (trans.), *The Odyssey*, Book XI, (London: Penguin, 1991), p. 160.

28. Lieut.-Col. John McCrae, MD, *In Flanders Fields and Other Poems* (Toronto: William Briggs, 1919), pp. 11–12.

29. C. Day-Lewis (trans.), *The Aeneid of Virgil*, Book VI (New York: Doubleday, Anchor, 1952), p. 133, lines 126–9. My own adaptation.

30. On this ceremonial money is usually printed the words, 'Hell Bank Note.'

31. As in the Elizabeth Marshall Thomas novel about prehistoric hunters, *Reindeer Moon* (New York: Pocket Books, 1991).

32. 1 Samuel 28: 15.

33. See the Other-Worldly arrangements in Ursula K. LeGuin, *A Wizard of Earthsea* (New York: Bantam, 1984).

34. See Farley Mowat, *People of the Deer* (Toronto: Bantam, 1984), also Carlo Ginzburg, Anne Tedeschi and John Tedeschi (trans.), *The Night Battles: Witchcraft and Agrarian Cults in the Sixteenth and Seventeenth Centuries* (Baltimore, MD: Johns Hopkins University Press, 1992).

35. 'Inanna's Journey to Hell,' *Poems of Heaven and Hell from Ancient Mesopotamia*, p. 145.

36. Jorge Luis Borges, Eliot Weinberger (ed., trans.), 'Nine Dantesque Essays 1945–1951,' *The Total Library: Non-Fiction 1922–1986* (London: Allen Lane, Penguin Press, 1999), pp. 267–305.

37. Ibid., p. 304. There are numerous examples of writers using their writing to retrieve a lost one. Three recent Canadian ones are: Graeme Gibson, *Gentlemen Death* (Toronto: McClelland and Stewart, 1995); Matt Cohen, *Last Seen* (Toronto: Vintage, 1996); Rudy Wiebe, 'Where is the Voice Coming From?,' Robert Weaver and Margaret Atwood (eds.), *The Oxford Book of Canadian Short Stories in English* (Toronto: Oxford University Press Canada, 1986).

38. Day-Lewis (trans.), *Aeneid*, Book VI, p. 137, lines 264–8.

39. See Italo Calvino's comment to the effect that shamanism is one of the functions of the writer in Patrick Creagh (trans.), *Six Memos for the Next Millennium* (Cambridge, MA: Harvard University Press, 1988).

40. Rilke, '9 [You have to have been among the shades],' *Sonnets to Orpheus*, Part I, p. 19.

41. N. K. Sandars (trans.), *The Epic of Gilgamesh* (London: Penguin, 1960, 1972), adapted from p. 177.

42. D. H. Lawrence, 'Bavarian Gentians,' *The Norton Anthology of Modern Poetry*, p. 372.

43. Gwendolyn MacEwen, 'Dark Pines Under Water,' *Gwendolyn MacEwen: The Early Years* (Toronto: Exile Editions, 1993), p. 156.

44. Adrienne Rich, 'Diving Into the Wreck,' *Diving into the Wreck* (New York: Norton, 1973).

45. Anne Hébert, 'The Tomb of the Kings,' Frank Scott (trans.), *Dialogue sur la Traduction* (Montreal: Editions HMH, 1970).

46. Wilfred Owen, Cecil Day-Lewis (ed.), 'Strange Meeting,' *Collected Poems of Wilfred Owen* (New York: New Directions, 1963).

47. Carlo Ginzburg, *Ecstacies: Deciphering the Witches' Sabbath* (NewYork: Penguin, 1991), p. 307.

48. Ovid, *Metamorphoses*, Mary Innes (trans.), (London: Penguin, 1955), p. 315.

Bibliography

Abé, Kobo. Saunders, E. Dale (trans.), *The Woman in the Dunes*
(New York: Vintage, 1964, 1972).

Akhmatova, Anna. Kunitz, Stanley and Hayward, Stanley (trans.),
Poems of Akhmatova (Boston: Atlantic Monthly Press, 1973).

Atwood, Margaret (ed.), *The New Oxford Book of Canadian Verse
in English* (Toronto: Oxford University Press Canada, 1982).

Austen, Jane. Tony Tanner (ed.), *Pride and Prejudice* (London:
Penguin, 1972).

Baudelaire, Charles. Roy Campbell (trans.), To the Reader,
Flowers of Evil (Norfolk, USA: New Directions, 1955).

Baum, L. Frank, *The Wizard of Oz* (London: Puffin, 1982).

Benjamin, Walter. Arendt, Hannah (ed.), 'The Work of Art in the
Age of Mechanical Reproduction' and 'The Storyteller,'
Illuminations (New York: Schocken Books, 1969).

Berlin, Isaiah. Hardy, Henry (ed.), *The Roots of Romanticism*
(Princeton University Press, 1999).

Birney, Earle, 'Yes, Canadians Can Read . . . But Do They?',
Canadian Home Journal, July, 1948.

Borges, Jorge Luis. James E. Irby (trans.), 'Borges and I,'
Everything and Nothing (New York: New Directions, 1999).

Weinberger, Eliot (ed.), Allen, Esther (trans.), 'Flaubert and
His Exemplary Destiny,' *The Total Library: Non-Fiction
1922–1986* (London: Allen Lane, Penguin Press, 1999).

Weinberger, Eliot (ed. and trans.), 'Nine Dantesque Essays

1945–1951' and 'Ray Bradbury: the Martian Chronicles,' *The Total Library: Non-Fiction 1922–1986* (London: Allen Lane, Penguin Press, 1999).

Bowen, Elizabeth, 'The Demon Lover,' *The Demon Lover and Other Stories* (London: Jonathan Cape, 1945).

Bradbury, Ray, 'The Martian,' *The Martian Chronicles* (New York: Bantam, 1977).

Fahrenheit 451 (New York: Ballantine Books, 1995).

Brown, E. K. and Bailey, J. O. (eds.), *Victorian Poetry* (New York: Ronald Press, 1962).

Brown, E. K. Smith, A. J. M., (ed.), 'The Problem of a Canadian Literature,' *Masks of Fiction: Canadian Critics on Canadian Prose* (Toronto: McClelland and Stewart, 1961).

Bulwer-Lytton, Edward, *Richelieu* (London: Saunders and Otley, 1839).

Bunyan, John. Sharrock, Roger (ed.), *The Pilgrim's Progress* (London: Penguin, 1987).

Burroughs, William S., *The Naked Lunch* (New York: Grove Press, 1992).

Calvino, Italo. Patrick Creagh (trans.), *Six Memos for the Next Millennium* (Cambridge, MA: Harvard University Press, 1988).

Canetti, Elias, *The Agony of Flies* (New York: Farrar, Straus, and Giroux, 1994).

Wedgwood, C. V. (trans.), *Auto da Fé* (London: Picador, Pan Books, 1978).

Carroll, Lewis, *Alice in Wonderland and Through the Looking Glass* (London: Collins, no copyright date given).

Chaucer, Geoffrey. Robinson, F. N. (ed.), *The Works of Geoffrey Chaucer* (London: Oxford University Press, 1957).

Chekhov, Anton. Hingley, Ronald (ed. and trans.), 'Lights,' *The Oxford Chekhov Volume IV: Stories 1888–1889* (Oxford University Press, 1980).

Child, Francis James (ed.), *The English and Scottish Popular Ballads* (New York: Dover, no copyright date given), vol. I.

Cohen, Matt, *Last Seen* (Toronto: Vintage, 1996).

Typing (Toronto: Knopf Canada, 2000).

Coleridge, Samuel Taylor, *The Rime of the Ancient Mariner and Other Poems* (New York: Dover, 1992).

Connolly, Cyril, *Enemies of Promise* (Harmondsworth, Middlesex: Penguin, 1961).

Davies, Robertson, *The Merry Heart: Robertson Davies Selections 1980–1995* (Toronto: McClelland and Stewart, 1996).

Day-Lewis, C. (trans.), *The Aeneid of Virgil* (New York: Doubleday, Anchor, 1952).

De Lillo, Don, *Mao II* (New York: Penguin, 1991).

Dickens, Charles, *The Old Curiosity Shop* (Ware, Hertfordshire: Wordsworth Editions, 1998).

Dickinson, Emily. Johnson, Thomas H. (ed.), *The Complete Poems of Emily Dickinson* (Boston: Little, Brown 1960).

Dinesen, Isak, 'Tempests,' *Anecdotes of Destiny* (London: Penguin, 1958).

  'A Consolatory Tale' and 'The Young Man With the Carnation,' *Winter's Tales* (New York: Vintage, 1993).

Doctorow, E. L., *City of God* (New York: Random House, 2000).

Duras, Marguerite. Polizzotti, Mark (trans.), *Writing* (Cambridge, MA: Lumen Editions, 1993).

Eliot, George, *Daniel Deronda* (Oxford University Press, 1988).

Ellmann, Richard and O'Clair, Robert (eds.), *The Norton Anthology of Modern Poetry*, Second Edition (New York: Norton, 1988).

Emerson, Ralph Waldo. Cook, Reginald L. (ed.), 'The Rhodora,' *Ralph Waldo Emerson: Selected Prose and Poetry* (New York: Rinehart, 1950).

Fielding, Henry, *Tom Jones* (New York: Signet, Penguin, 1963, 1979)

Gallant, Mavis, Preface and 'A Painful Affair,' *The Selected Short Stories of Mavis Gallant* (Toronto: McClelland and Stewart, 1996).

Gautier, Théophile, Preface, *Mademoiselle de Maupin* (New York: Modern Library, 1920).

Gay, Peter, *The Pleasure Wars* (New York: Norton, 1998).

Gibson, Graeme, *Gentlemen Death* (Toronto: McClelland and Stewart, 1995).

Ginzburg, Carlo. Rosenthal, Raymond (trans.), *Ecstasies: Deciphering the Witches' Sabbath* (New York: Penguin, 1991).
  Tedeschi, Anne and Tedeschi, John (trans.), *The Night Battles: Witchcraft and Agrarian Cults in the Sixteenth and Seventeenth Centuries* (Baltimore, MD: Johns Hopkins University Press, 1992).

Gissing, George. Taylor, D. J. (ed.), *New Grub Street* (London: Everyman, 1997).

Glendinning, Victoria, *Edith Sitwell* (London: Phoenix, 1981).

Glück, Louise, *The House on Marshland* (Hopewell, NJ: Ecco Press, 1975).

Gordimer, Nadine, Introduction, *Selected Stories* (London: Bloomsbury, 2000).

Graves, Robert, *The White Goddess: A Historical Grammar of Poetic Myth* (London: Faber and Faber, 1952).

Greene, Graham, *The End of the Affair* (New York: Penguin, 1999).

Greer, Germaine, *Slip-Shod Sibyls: Recognition, Rejection and the Woman Poet* (London: Penguin, 1995).

Grimm, Brothers. Padraic Colum (intro.), 'The Robber Bridegroom,' 'The Goose Girl,' and 'The Singing Bone,' *The Complete Grimms' Fairy Tales* (New York: Pantheon, 1972).

Harvey, William Fryer, *The Beast with Five Fingers* (New York: Dutton, 1947).

Hébert, Anne. Scott, Frank (trans.), 'The Tomb of Kings,' *Dialogue sur la Traduction* (Montreal: Editions HMH, 1970).

Hewlett, Maurice, *The Forest Lovers* (London, Macmillan, 1899).

The Holy Bible

Homer. Rieu, E. V. (trans.), *The Odyssey* (London: Penguin, 1991).

Hrabal, Bohumile. Michael Henry Heim (trans.), *Too Loud a Solitude* (London: Abacus, 1990).

Hunt, Leigh. Jesson-Dibley, David (ed.), *Selected Writings* (Manchester: Fyfield Books, 1990).

Hyde, Lewis, *The Gift: Imagination and the Erotic Life of Property* (New York: Vintage, Random House, 1983).

Il Postino. Written by Troisi, Massimo et al., directed by Radford, Michael. Miramax Home Entertainment, 1995.

Ingelow, Jean, *Mopsa the Fairy* (London: J. M. Dent, no copyright date given).

Irving, John, *A Widow for One Year* (Toronto: Alfred A. Knopf, 1998).

James, Henry, 'The Death of the Lion,' and 'The Lesson of the Master,' *The Lesson of the Master and Other Stories* (London: John Lehmann, 1948).

   'The Author of *Beltraffiio*,' *In the Cage and Other Tales* (London: Rupert Hart Davis, 1958).

   The Sacred Fount (New York: New Directions, 1995).

Joyce, James, *A Portrait of the Artist As a Young Man* (New York: Penguin, 1993).

Kafka, Franz. Pasley, Malcolm (ed. and trans.), 'A Fasting-Artist' and 'In the Penal Colony,' *The Transformation and Other Stories* (London: Penguin, 1992).

Keats, John. Bush, Douglas (ed.), *Selected Poems and Letters* (Cambridge, MA: Riverside Press, 1959).

King, Stephen, *Misery* (New York: Viking, Penguin, 1987).

Klein, A. M., *The Rocking Chair and Other Poems* (Toronto: Ryerson Press, 1966).

Lawrence, D. H., *Look We Have Come Through!* (New York: B. W. Huebsc, 1920).

Lawrence, D. H. Alberto Manguel (ed.), 'The Rocking-Horse Winner,' *Black Water: The Anthology of Fantastic Literature* (Toronto: Lester and Orpen Dennys, 1983).

Layton, Irving, Foreword, *A Red Carpet for the Sun* (Toronto: McClelland and Stewart, 1959).

Le Carré, John, *Smiley's People* (New York: Bantam, 1974).

LeGuin, Ursula K., *A Wizard of Earthsea* (New York: Bantam, 1984).

   The Telling (New York: Harcourt, 2000).

Leonard, Elmore, *Get Shorty* (New York: Delta, Dell, 1990).

Leroux, Gaston, *The Phantom of the Opera* (New York: HarperCollins, 1988).

Levi, Primo, *The Periodic Table* (New York: Schocken Books, 1984).

Rosenthal, Raymond (trans.), *The Drowned and the Saved* (London: Abacus, 1999).

Lévi-Strauss, Claude and Doniger, Wendy, *Myth and Meaning* (New York: Schocken Books, 1995).

MacDonald, Ann-Marie, *Fall on Your Knees* (Toronto: Alfred A. Knopf, 1996).

MacEwen, Gwendolyn, *Julian the Magician* (Toronto: Macmillan, 1963).

The Rising Fire (Toronto: Contact Editions, 1963) .

Breakfast for Barbarians (Toronto: Ryerson Press, 1966) .

Gwendolyn MacEwen: The Early Years (Toronto: Exile Editions, 1993).

Atwood, Margaret and Callaghan, Barry (eds.), Introduction by Rosemary Sullivan, *The Poetry of Gwendolyn MacEwen: The Later Years* (Toronto: Exile Editions, 1994).

MacLeish, Archibald, *Collected Poems 1917–1982* (Boston: Houghton Mifflin, 1985).

Macpherson, Jay, *Poems Twice Told: The Boatman and Welcoming Disaster* (Toronto: Oxford University Press, 1981).

McEwan, Ian, 'Reflections of a Kept Ape,' *In Between the Sheets* (London: Jonathan Cape, 1978).

McRobbie, Kenneth, *Eyes Without A Face* (Toronto: Gallery Editions, 1960).

Malleus Maleficarum or *Hexenhammer* (1484).

Mandelstam, Osip, *Selected Poems* (New York: Farrar, Straus, and Giroux, 1975).

Mann, Klaus, *Mephisto* (Hamburg: Rowohlt Taschenbuch Verlag, 1980).

Michaels, Anne, *Miner's Pond, The Weight of Oranges, Skin Divers* (London: Bloomsbury, 2000).

Milton, John, *Paradise Lost* (London: Penguin, 2000).

Mitford, Nancy, *Voltaire in Love* (London: Hamish Hamilton, 1957).

Moore, Brian, *An Answer from Limbo* (Boston: Atlantic, Little, Brown, 1992).

Mowat, Farley, *People of the Deer* (Toronto: Bantam, 1984).

Munro, Alice, 'Material,' *Something I've Been Meaning To Tell You* (Toronto: McGraw Hill Ryerson, 1974).

Who Do You Think You Are? (Agincourt, ONT.: Signet, 1978).

'Cortes Island,' *The Love of a Good Woman* (Toronto: Penguin, 1999).

Ondaatje, Michael, *Anil's Ghost* (Toronto: McClelland and Stewart, 2000).

Orwell, George, *Nineteen Eighty-Four* (Harmondsworth, Middlesex: Penguin, 1949).

'Why I Write,' *The Penguin Essays of George Orwell* (London: Penguin, 1968).

Ovid. Innes, Mary (trans.) *Metamorphoses* (London: Penguin, 1955).

Owen, Wilfred. Day-Lewis, Cecil (ed.), *Collected Poems of Wilfred Owen* (New York: New Directions, 1963).

Petiska, Eduard and Svábová, Jana (trans.), *Golem* (Prague: Martin, 1991).

Plath, Sylvia, *The Collected Poems* (New York: Harper and Row, 1981).

Poe, Edgar Allan, 'The Purloined Letter,' *Selected Writings of Edgar Allan Poe* (Boston: Houghton Mifflin Company, 1956).

Purdy, Al, *Beyond Remembering: The Collected Poems of Al Purdy* (Madeira Park, BC: Harbour Publishing, 2000).

Pushkin, Alexander. Yarmolinsky, Avraham (ed.), *The Poems, Prose and Plays of Alexander Pushkin* (New York: The Modern Library, 1936).

Reaney, James. A. J. M. Smith (ed.), 'The Canadian Poet's Predicament,' *Masks of Poetry: Canadian Critics on Canadian Verse* (Toronto: McClelland and Stewart, 1962).

Atwood, Margaret and Weaver, Robert (eds.), 'The Bully,' *The Oxford Book of Canadian Short Stories in English* (Toronto: Oxford University Press Canada, 1986).

Rich, Adrienne, *Diving Into the Wreck* (New York: Norton, 1973).

Rilke, Rainer Maria. Young, David (trans.), *Sonnets to Orpheus* (Hanover, NH: Wesleyan University Press, 1987).

Rostand, Edmond, *Cyrano de Bergerac* (New York: Bantam, 1954).

Sandars, N. K. (trans.), *Poems of Heaven and Hell from Ancient Mesopotamia* (London: Penguin Classics, 1971).

The Epic of Gilgamesh (London: Penguin, 1972).

Sebald, W. G. Hulse, Michael (trans.), *Vertigo* (New York: New Directions, 2000).

Shakespeare, William. Greenblatt, Stephen (ed.), *King Richard III, The Complete Works of William Shakespeare* (New York: Norton, 1997).

Macbeth, The Complete Works of William Shakespeare (New York: Norton, 1997).

The Tempest, The Complete Works of William Shakespeare (New York: Norton, 1997).

King Henry the Fifth, The Complete Works of William Shakespeare (New York: Norton, 1997).

Hamlet, The Complete Works of William Shakespeare (New York: Norton, 1997).

King Lear, The Complete Works of William Shakespeare (New York: Norton, 1997).

Shelley, Percy Bysshe. Reiman, Donald H. and Powers, Sharon B. (eds.), *Shelley's Poetry and Prose: Authoritative Texts, Criticism* (New York: Norton, 1977).

Shields, Carol, *Swann: A Mystery* (Toronto: Stoddart, 1987).

Smith, A. J. M. (ed.), *The Book of Canadian Poetry: A Critical and Historical Anthology* (Toronto: W. J. Gage, 1957).

Söderberg, Hjalmar. Austin, Paul Britten (trans.), *Doctor Glas* (London: Tandem, 1963).

Stein, Gertrude, *Four Saints in Three Acts, Gertrude Stein: Writings 1903–1932* (New York: Library of America, 1998).

Tertz, Abram, 'The Icicle,' *The Icicle and Other Stories* (London: Collins and Harvill, 1963)

Thackeray, W. M., *Vanity Fair* (London: J. M. Dent and Sons, 1957).

Thomas, Elizabeth Marshall, *Reindeer Moon* (New York: Pocket Books, 1991).

Tierney, Patrick, *The Highest Altar* (New York: Viking, 1989).

Tymms, Ralph, *Doubles in Literary Psychology* (Oxford: Bowes and Bowes, 1949).

Villon, François. Kinnell, Galway (ed.), *The Poems of François Villon* (Boston: Houghton Mifflin, 1965,1977).

Von Chiamisso, Adelbert, *Peter Schlemihl* (London: Camden House, 1993).

Weaver, Robert and Toye, William (eds.), *The Oxford Anthology of Canadian Literature* (Toronto: Oxford University Press Canada, 1973).

Welty, Eudora; 'The Petrified Man,' *Selected Stories of Eudora Welty* (New York: The Modern Library, 1936, 1943).

Wiebe, Rudy. Atwood, Margaret and Weaver, Robert (eds.), 'Where is the Voice Coming From?,' *The Oxford Book of Canadian Short Stories in English* (Toronto: Oxford University Press, 1986).

Wilde, Oscar, *The Picture of Dorian Gray* (Ware, Hertfordshire: Wordsworth Editions, 1992).

Wilson, Milton. Smith, A. J. M. (ed.), 'Other Canadians and After,' *Masks of Fiction: Canadian Critics on Canadian Prose* (Toronto: McClelland and Stewart, 1961).

Woods, George Benjamin and Buckley, Jerome Hamilton (eds.), *Poetry of the Victorian Period* (Chicago: Scott, Foresman, 1955).

Wordsworth, William. Gill, Stephen and Wu, Duncan (eds.), *William Wordsworth: Selected Poetry* (Oxford University Press, 1998).

Yeats, William Butler, *The Collected Poems of W. B. Yeats: Last Poems* (London: Macmillan, 1961).

Young, Dudley, *Origins of the Sacred: The Ecstasies of Love and War* (New York: St. Martin's Press, 1991).

Acknowledgments

We would like thank the following for their kind permission to reprint the work contained in this volume. Every attempt has been made to contact copyright holders of remaining texts; our apologies to any whom we have inadvertently missed.

Joan Acocella, *The New Yorker*.

Milton Acorn, *Dig Up My Heart: Selected Poems*, McClelland & Stewart Ltd.

Jorge Luis Borges, 'Everything and Nothing' from *Labyrinths*, copyright © 1962, 1964 by New Directions Publishing Corp. Reprinted by permission of New Directions Publishing Corp.; *The Total Library Non-Fiction, 1922–1986* edited Eliot Weinberger, trans. Esther Allen, Suzanne Jill Levine, and Eliot Weinberger, copyright © Esther Allen, © Suzanne Jill Levine, © Eliot Weinberger, 1999. Reprinted by permission of Allen Lane and The Penguin Press, 2000.

Ray Bradbury, *The Martian Chronicles*, copyright © 1950, renewed 1977 by Ray Bradbury. Reprinted by permission of Don Congdon Associates, Inc.

Elias Canetti, *Auto da fé*. Reprinted by permission of Jonathan Cape and The Random House Group Ltd.

Cyril Connolly, *Enemies of Promise*. Reprinted by permission of A. J. Monsey for Rogers, Coleridge & White Ltd. on behalf of the Estate of Cyril Connolly.

Robertson Davies, *The Merry Heart*. Reprinted by permission of McClelland & Stewart Ltd., and Pendragon Ink.

Isak Dinesen, *Winter's Tales,* copyright © 1942 by Random House, Inc., renewed 1970 by Johan Philip Thomas Ingerslev; *Anecdotes of Destiny,* copyright © 1958 by Isak Dinesen, renewed by the Rungstedlund Foundation. Reprinted by permission of Rungstedlund Foundation and Michael Joseph.

E. L. Doctorow, *City of God*. Reprinted by permission of the author.

Mavis Gallant, *Selected Stories*. Reprinted by permission of McClelland & Steward, Ltd. and Georges Borchardt, Inc. Literary Agency.

Peter Gay, *The Pleasure Wars*, W. W. Norton.

Carlo Ginzburg, *Ecstacies: Deciphering the Witches' Sabbath*. Reprinted by permission of Einaudi Editore and The Bobbe Siegel Literary Agency.

Nadine Gordimer, *Selected Stories*. Reprinted by permission of the author.

Graham Greene, *The End of the Affair*, copyright © 1951, renewed © 1979 by Graham Greene. Reprinted by permission of Viking Penguin, a division of Penguin Putnam and The Random House Group Ltd.

Daryl Hine, 'The Doppelgänger.' *The Oxford Book of Canadian Verse*. Reprinted by permission of the author.

Homer, *The Odyssey*, E.V. Rieu trans., revised translation D. C. H. Rieu, 1946, 1991, copyright © 1946 by E.V. Rieu, this revised translation copyright © the Estate of the late E.V. Rieu and D. C. H. Rieu, 1991. Reprinted by permission of Penguin Classics.

John Irving, *A Widow for One Year*. Reprinted by permission of the author.

Franz Kafka, *The Transformation and Other Stories*, Malcolm Pasley trans., copyright © Malcolm Pasley, 1992. Reprinted by permission of Penguin Classics.

Galway Kinnell, *The Collected Poems of François Villon*, copyright © 1965, 1977 by Galway Kinnell. Reprinted by permission of Houghton Mifflin and Company.

D. H . Lawrence, *The Complete Poems of D. H. Lawrence*. Reprinted by permission of Laurence Pollinger Ltd. and the Estate of Frieda Lawrence Ravagli.

Irving Layton, *A Red Carpet for the Sun*. Reprinted by permission of McClelland & Stewart Ltd. and M. Schwartz.

Primo Levi, *The Periodic Table*, English trans., copyright © 1984 Schocken Books, Italian text copyright © 1975 Einaudi. Reprinted by permission of Schocken Books.

C. Day Lewis, *The Aenid of Virgil*. Reprinted by permission of Random House Inc. and The Peters Fraser & Dunlop Group Ltd.

Ann-Marie MacDonald, *Fall on Your Knees*. Reprinted by permission of the author.

Gwendolyn MacEwen, 'The Left Hand and Hiroshima' from *Breakfast for Barbarian*; 'Dark Pines Under Water' from *Gwendolyn MacEwen: the Early Years; The Poetry of Gwendolyn MacEwen: the Later Years; Julian the Magician*. Reprinted by permission of Exile Editions.

Archibald MacLeish, *Collected Poems*, Houghton Mifflin Company.

Jay Macpherson, 'Book' and 'The Well,' *The Oxford Anthology of Canadian Literature*, Oxford University Press.

Nancy Mitford, *Voltaire in Love*. Reprinted by permission of The Peters Fraser & Dunlop Group.

Alice Munro, *The Love of a Good Woman, Something I've Been Meaning To Tell You, Who Do you Think You Are?* Reprinted by permission of the author.

George Orwell, *1984*, and *Why I Write*, A. M. Heath & Co. Ltd., on behalf of Bill Hamilton as the Literary Executor of the estate of the late Sonia Brownell Orwell and Martin Secker & Warburg Ltd.

Sylvia Plath, *Collected Poems*, Faber and Faber Ltd.

Al Purdy, *Beyond Remembering: the Collected Poems of Al Purdy*, Harbour Publishing.

Adrienne Rich, the lines from 'Diving into the Wreck,' the lines from 'From the Prison House,' from *Diving into the Wreck: Poems 1971–1972* by Adrienne Rich. Copyright © 1973 by W. W. Norton & Company, Inc.

Rainer Maria Rilke, *Sonnets to Orpheus*, David Young trans. Reprinted by permission of Wesleyan University Press.

N. K. Sandars trans., *The Epic of Gilgamesh*, third edition, copyright © N. K. Sandars, 1960, 1964, 1972; *Poems of Heaven and Hell from Ancient Mesopotamia*, copyright © N. K. Sandars, 1971. Reprinted by permission of Penguin Classics.

Danny Shanahan, 'The moving finger writes, and having writ moves on to a three-week, twenty-city book tour.' Reprinted by permission of *The New Yorker*.

Gertrude Stein, *The Collected Works*, Library of America.

Eudora Welty, *The Selected Stories of Eudora Welty*, Harcourt Brace and Co.

Milton Wilson, 'Other Canadians and After' from *Masks of Fiction: Canadian Critics on Canadian Verse*. Reprinted by permission of the author.

Index